Human Language Technologies: The 2010 Annual Conference of the North American Chapter of the Association for Computational Linguistics (NAACL HLT 2010)

Demonstration Session

Los Angeles, California, USA
2 June 2010

ISBN: 978-1-61738-708-1

Printed from e-media with permission by:

Curran Associates, Inc.
57 Morehouse Lane
Red Hook, NY 12571

Some format issues inherent in the e-media version may also appear in this print version.

Printed by Curran Associates, Inc. (2010)

For permission requests, please contact the Association for Computational Linguistics at the address below.

Association for Computational Linguistics
209 N. Eighth Street
Stroudsburg, Pennsylvania 18360

Phone: 1-570-476-8006
Fax: 1-570-476-0860

acl@aclweb.org

Additional copies of this publication are available from:

Curran Associates, Inc.
57 Morehouse Lane
Red Hook, NY 12571 USA
Phone: 845-758-0400
Fax: 845-758-2634
Email: curran@proceedings.com
Web: www.proceedings.com

Table of Contents

Demonstrations Program

Wednesday, June 2, 2010

Poster and Demo Plenary Session

4:10–5:30 One-Minute Madness: Poster and Demo Previews

5:30–6:30 **Break**

6:30–8:30 **Demonstration Session**

Camtology: Intelligent Information Access for Science
Ted Briscoe, Karl Harrison, Andrew Naish-Guzman, Andy Parker, Advaith Siddharthan, David Sinclair, Mark Slater and Rebecca Watson

Summarizing Textual Information about Locations In a Geo-Spatial Information Display System
Congxing Cai and Eduard Hovy

Phrasal: A Statistical Machine Translation Toolkit for Exploring New Model Features
Daniel Cer, Michel Galley, Daniel Jurafsky and Christopher D. Manning

Multilingual Propbank Annotation Tools: Cornerstone and Jubilee
Jinho Choi, Claire Bonial and Martha Palmer

KSC-PaL: A Peer Learning Agent that Encourages Students to take the Initiative
Cynthia Kersey, Barbara Di Eugenio, Pamela Jordan and Sandra Katz

A Detailed, Accurate, Extensive, Available English Lexical Database
Adam Kilgarriff

An Interactive Tool for Supporting Error Analysis for Text Mining
Elijah Mayfield and Carolyn Penstein Rosé

Serious Game Environments for Language and Culture Education
Alicia Sagae, W. Lewis Johnson and Rebecca Row

Interpretation of Partial Utterances in Virtual Human Dialogue Systems
Kenji Sagae, David DeVault and David Traum

Camtology: Intelligent Information Access for Science

Ted Briscoe[1,2], Karl Harrison[5], Andrew Naish-Guzman[4], Andy Parker[1], Advaith Siddharthan[3], David Sinclair[4], Mark Slater[5] and Rebecca Watson[2]

[1]University of Cambridge
ejb1@cl.cam.ac.uk,
parker@hep.phy.cam.ac.uk,

[2]iLexIR Ltd
rfw@ilexir.co.uk
[3]University of Aberdeen
advaith@abdn.ac.uk

[4]Camtology Ltd
david.sinclair@imense.co.uk,
a.naish@gmail.com

[5]University of Birmingham
kh@hep.ph.bham.ac.uk,
mws@hep.ph.bham.ac.uk

Abstract

We describe a novel semantic search engine for scientific literature. The Camtology system allows for sentence-level searches of PDF files and combines text and image searches, thus facilitating the retrieval of information present in tables and figures. It allows the user to generate complex queries for search terms that are related through particular grammatical/semantic relations in an intuitive manner. The system uses Grid processing to parallelise the analysis of large numbers of papers.

1 Introduction

Scientific, technological, engineering and medical (STEM) research is entering the so-called 4th Paradigm of "data-intensive scientific discovery", in which advanced data mining and pattern discovery techniques need to be applied to vast datasets in order to drive further discoveries. A key component of this process is efficient search and exploitation of the huge repository of information that only exists in textual or visual form within the "bibliome", which itself continues to grow exponentially.

Today's computationally driven research methods have outgrown traditional methods of searching for scientific data, creating a widespread and unfulfilled need for advanced search and information extraction. Camtology combines text and image processing to create a unique solution to this problem.

2 Status

Camtology has developed a search and information extraction system which is currently undergoing usability testing with the curation team for FlyBase[1], a $1m/year NIH-funded curated database covering the functional genomics of the fruit fly. To provide a scalable solution capable of analysing the entire STEM bibliome of over 20m electronic journal and conference papers, we have developed a robust system that can be used with a grid of computers running distributed job management software.

This system has been deployed and tested using a subset of the resources provided by the UK Grid for Particle Physics (Britton et al., 2009), part of the worldwide Grid of around 200000 CPU cores assembled to allow analysis of the petabyte-scale data volumes to be recorded each year by experiments at the Large Hadron Collider in Geneva. Processing of the FlyBase archive of around 15000 papers required about 8000 hours of CPU time, and has been successfully completed in about 3 days, with up to a few hundred jobs run in parallel. A distributed spider for collecting open-source PDF documents has also been developed. This has been run concurrently on over 2000 cores cores, and has been used to retrieve over 350000 subject-specific papers, but these are not considered in the present demo.

3 Functionality

Camtology's search and extraction engine is the first to integrate a full structural analysis of a scientific paper in PDF format (identifying headings, sections, captions and associated figures, citations and references) with a sentence-by-sentence grammatical analysis of the text and direct visual search over figures. Combining these capabilities allows us to transform paper search from keyword based paper retrieval, where the end result is a set of putatively relevant PDF files which need to be read, to information extraction based on the ability to interactively specify a rich variety of linguistic patterns which return sentences in specific document locales, and which combine text with image-based constraints; for instance:

> "all sentences in figure captions which contain any gene name as the theme of the action 'express' where the figure is a picture of an eye"

[1]http://flybase.org/

Proceedings of the NAACL HLT 2010: Demonstration Session, pages 1–4,
Los Angeles, California, June 2010.

Camtology allows the user to build up such complex queries quickly though an intuitive process of query refinement.

Figures often convey information crucial to the understanding of the content of a paper and are typically not available to search. Camtology's search engine integrates text search to the figure and caption level with the ability to re-rank search returns on the basis of visual similarity to a chosen archetype (ambiguities in textual relevance are often resolved by visual appearance). Figure 1 provides a compact overview of the search functionality supported by our current demonstrator. Interactively, constructing and running such complex queries takes a few seconds in our intuitive user interface, and allows the user to quickly browse and then aggregate information across the entire collection of papers indexed by the system. For instance, saving the search result from the example above would yield a computer-readable list of gene names involved in eye development (in fruit flies in our demonstrator) in a second or so. With existing web portals and keyword based selection of PDF files (for example, Google Scholar, ScienceDirect, DeepDyve or PubGet), a query like this would typically take many hours to open and read each one, using cut and paste to extract gene names (and excludes the possibility of ordering results on a visual basis). The only other alternative would require expensive bespoke adaptation of a text mining system by IT professionals using licensed software (such as Ariadne Genomics, Temis or Linguamatics). This option is only available to a tiny minority of researchers working for large well-funded corporations.

4 Summary of Technology

4.1 PDF to SciXML

The PDF format represents a document in a manner designed to facilitate printing. In short, it provides information on font and position for textual and graphical units. To enable information retrieval and extraction, we need to convert this typographic representation into a logical one that reflects the structure of scientific documents. We use an XML schema called SciXML (first introduced in Teufel et al. (1999)) that we extend to include images. We linearise the textual elements in the PDF, representing these as <div> elements in XML and classify these divisions as {Title|Author|Affiliation|Abstract|Footnote|Caption|Heading|Citation| References|Text} in a constraint satisfaction framework.

In addition, we identify all graphics in the PDF, including lines and images. We then identify tables by looking for specific patterns of text and lines. A bounding box is identified for a table and an image is generated that overlays the text on the lines. Similarly we overlay text onto images that have been identified and identify bounding boxes for figures. This representation allows us to retrieve figures and tables that consist of text and graphics. Once bounding boxes for tables or figures have been identified, we identify a one-to-one association between captions and boxes that minimises the total distance between captions and their associated figures or tables. The image is then referenced from the caption using a "SRC" attribute; for example, in (abbreviated for space constraints):

<CAPTION SRC= "FBrf0174566_fig_6_o.png"> <b>Fig. 6. </b> Phenotypic analysis of denticle belt fusions during embryogenesis. (A) The denticle belt fusion phenotype resulted in folds around the surrounding fused... ...(G) ...the only cuticle phenotype of the DN-EGFR-expressing embryos was strong denticle belt fusions in alternating parasegments (<i>paired </i>domains).</CAPTION>

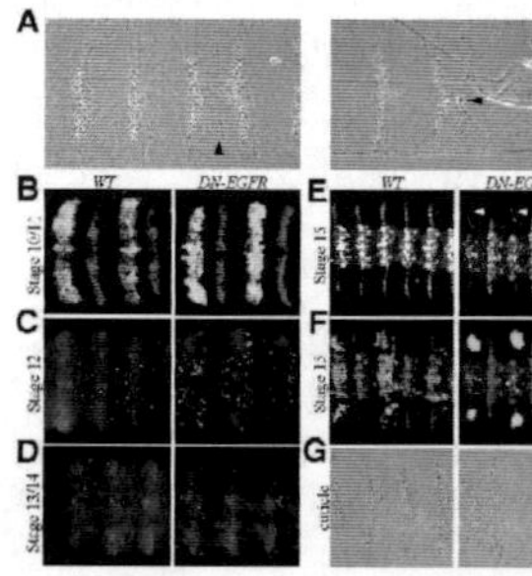

Note how informative the caption is, and the value of being able to search this caption in conjunction with the corresponding image (also shown above).

4.2 Natural Language Processing

Every sentence, including those in abstracts, titles and captions, is run through our named-entity recogniser and syntactic parser. The output of these systems is then indexed, enabling semantic search.

Named Entity Recognition

NER in the biomedical domain was implemented as described in Vlachos (2007). Gene Mention tagging was performed using Conditional Random Fields and syntactic parsing, using features derived from grammatical relations to augment the tagging. We also use a probabilistic model for resolution of non-pronominal anaphora in biomedical texts. The model focuses on biomedical entities and seeks to find the antecedents of anaphora, both coreferent and associative ones, and also to identify discourse-new expressions (Gasperin and Briscoe, 2008).

Parsing

The RASP toolkit (Briscoe et al., 2006) is used for sentence boundary detection, tokenisation, PoS tagging and finding grammatical relations (GR) between words in the text. GRs are triplets consisting of a relation-type and two arguments and also encode morphology, word position and part-of-speech; for example, parsing "John likes Mary." gives us a subject relation and a direct object relation:

(|ncsubj| |like+s:2_VVZ| |John:1_NP1|)
(|dobj| |like+s:2_VVZ| |Mary:3_NP1|)

Representing a parse as a set of flat triplets allows us to index on grammatical relations, thus enabling complex relational queries.

4.3 Image Processing

We build a low-dimensional feature vector to summarise the content of each extracted image. Colour and intensity histograms are encoded in a short bit string which describes the image globally; this is concatenated with a description of the image derived from a wavelet decomposition (Jacobs et al., 1995) that captures finer-scale edge information. Efficient similar image search is achieved by projecting these feature vectors onto a small number of randomly-generated hyperplanes and using the signs of the projections as a key for locality-sensitive hashing (Gionis et al., 1999).

4.4 Indexing and Search

We use Lucene (Goetz, 2002) for indexing and retrieving sentences and images. Lucene is an open source indexing and information retrieval library that has been shown to scale up efficiently and handle large numbers of queries. We index using fields derived from word-lemmas, grammatical relations and named entities. At the same time, these complex representations are hidden from the user, who, as a first step, performs a simple keyword search; for example "express Vnd". This returns all sentences that contain the words "express" and "Vnd" (search is on lemmatised words, so morphological variants of "express" will be retrieved). Different colours represent different types of biological entities and processes (green for a gene), and blue shows the entered search terms in the result sentences. An example sentence retrieved for the above query follows:

> It is possible that like ac , sc and l'sc , vnd is expressed initially in cell clusters and then restricted to single cells .

Next, the user can select specific words in the returned sentences to indirectly specify a relation. Clicking on a word will select it, indicated by underlining of the word. In the example above, the words "vnd" and "expressed" have been selected by the user. This creates a new query that returns sentences where "vnd" is the subject of "express" and the clause is in passive voice. This retrieval is based on a sophisticated grammatical analysis of the text, and can retrieve sentences where the words in the relation are far apart. An example of a sentence retrieved for the refined query is shown below:

> First , vnd might be spatially regulated in a manner similar to ac and sc and selectively expressed in these clusters .

Camtology offers two other functionalities. The user can browse the MeSH (Medical Subject Headings) ontology and retrieve papers relevant to a MeSH term. Also, for both search and MeSH browsing, retrieved papers are plotted on a world map; this is done by converting the affiliations of the authors into geospatial coordinates. The user can then directly access papers from a particular site.

5 Script Outline

I Quick overview of existing means of searching science (PubMed, FlyBase, Google Scholar).

II Walk through the functionality of Camtology (these are numbered in Figure 1:

- (1) Initial query through textual search box; (2) Retrieval of relevant sentences; (3) Query refinement by clicking on words; (4) Using implicit grammatical relations for new search;
- Alternative to search: (5) Browse MeSH Ontology to retrieve papers with MeSH terms.
- (6) Specifically searching for tables/figures
- (7) Viewing the affiliation of the authors of retrieved papers on a world map.
- (8) Image search using similarity of image.

6 Acknowledgements

This work was supported in part by a STFC miniPIPSS grant to the University of Cambridge and iLexIR Ltd.

References

T. Briscoe, J. Carroll, and R. Watson. 2006. The second release of the RASP system. In *Proc. ACL 2006*.

D. Britton, AJ Cass, PEL Clarke, et al. 2009. GridPP: the UK grid for particle physics. *Philosophical Transactions A*, 367(1897):2447.

C. Gasperin and T. Briscoe. 2008. Statistical anaphora resolution in biomedical texts. In *Proc. COLING'08*.

A. Gionis, P. Indyk, and R. Motwani. 1999. Similarity search in high dimensions via hashing. In *Proc. 25th ACM Internat. Conf. on Very Large Data Bases*.

B. Goetz. 2002. The Lucene search engine: Powerful, flexible, and free. *Javaworld http://www. javaworld. com/javaworld/jw-09-2000/jw-0915-lucene. html*.

C.E. Jacobs, A. Finkelstein, and D.H. Salesin. 1995. Fast multiresolution image querying. In *Proc. 22nd ACM annual conference on Computer graphics and interactive techniques*.

S. Teufel, J. Carletta, and M. Moens. 1999. An annotation scheme for discourse-level argumentation in research articles. In *Proc. EACL'99*.

A. Vlachos. 2007. Tackling the BioCreative2 gene mention task with CRFs and syntactic parsing. In *Proc. 2nd BioCreative Challenge Evaluation Workshop*.

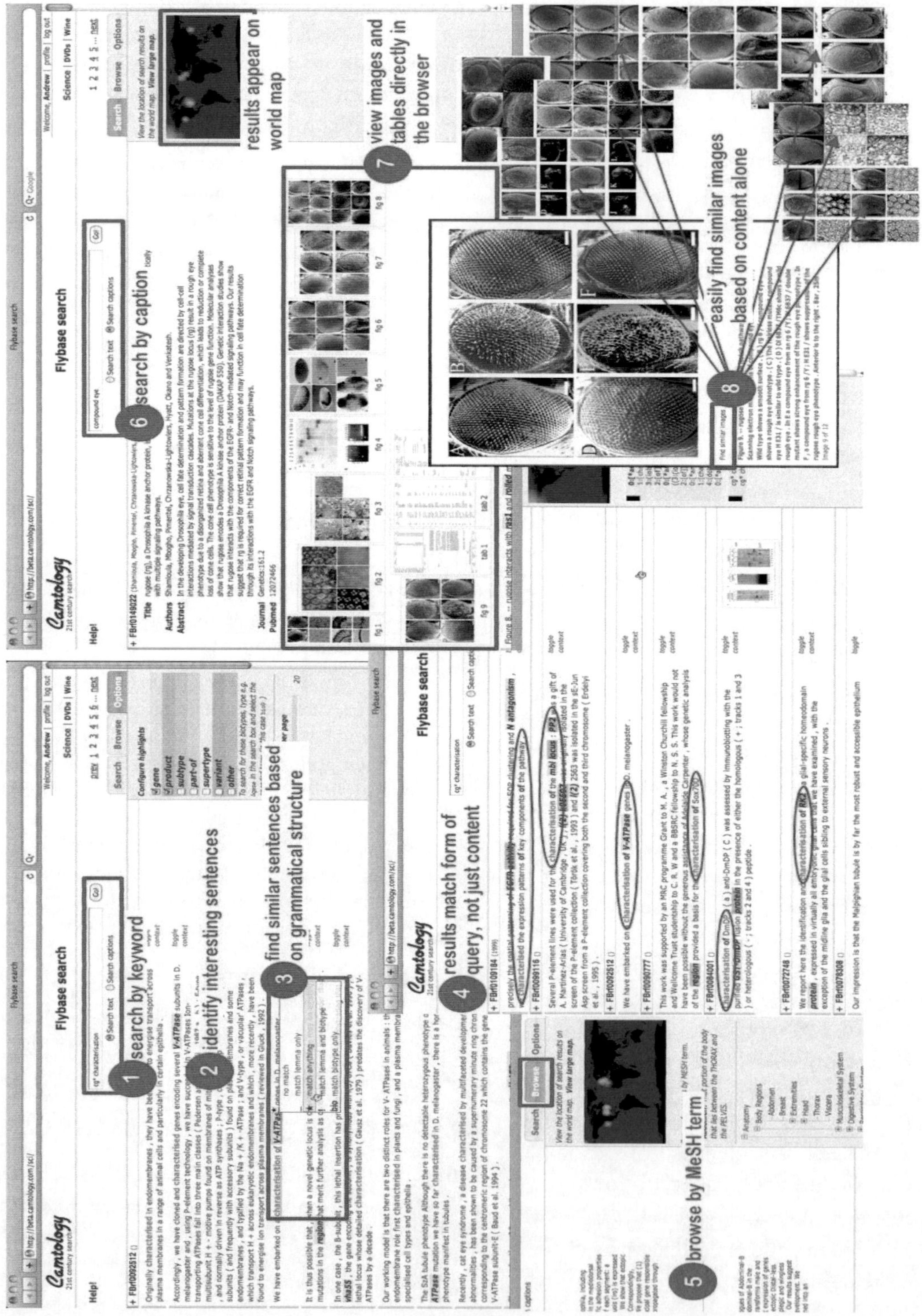

Figure 1: Screenshots showing functionality of the Camtology search engine.

Summarizing Textual Information about Locations In a Geo-Spatial Information Display System

Congxing Cai
Information Sciences Institute
University of Southern California
Marina del Rey, California, USA 90292
ccai@isi.edu

Eduard Hovy
Information Sciences Institute
University of Southern California
Marina del Rey, California, USA 90292
hovy@isi.edu

Abstract

This demo describes the summarization of textual material about locations in the context of a geo-spatial information display system. When the amount of associated textual data is large, it is organized and summarized before display. A hierarchical summarization framework, conditioned on the small space available for display, has been fully implemented. Snapshots of the system, with narrative descriptions, demonstrate our results.

1 Introduction

Geospatial display systems are increasingly gaining attention, given the large amounts of geospatial data and services available online. Although geospatial imagery and maps show geometric relations among entities, they cannot be used to present other kinds of knowledge about the temporal, topic, and other conceptual relations and entities. Given an entity on a map, a description of what happened there, in what order in time, when, and why, requires additional types of information, typically contained in text, in order to support varied search and decision tasks.

In this demo, we apply text summarization to a geo-spatial information display system with potentially large amounts of textual data. By summarizing the textual material linked to each location, we demonstrate the ways one can organize this material for optimal display and search.

Of the many different types of text-oriented resources available, some are structured and others unstructured. This textual data can be linked to locations based on different reasons (containing place names, addresses, real objects with geographical features, etc.). Appropriately grouping and presenting the different aspects of the textual information in summarization is a challenging task.

A second challenge stems from the huge amounts of web material related to some geographical objects. For example, one may find millions of pages for a famous place or event at a specific map location. Given the common limitations of display space in most geospatial display systems, one must also design the interface to support dynamic browsing and search.

All these challenges bring new problems to existing summarization techniques. In the following sections, we demonstrate a hierarchical summarization framework that reduces displayed text and fully utilizes the small display space available for textual information.

2 Related Work

Associating each news page individually to its location(s) may overwhelm the amount of information displayable at any point and thereby limit the scalability of the system. Existing systems presented in (Teitler et al., 2008) and GeoTracker (Chen et al, 2007) organize material (at the area level) by time instead of somehow aggregating over larger numbers of related content. Since frequently the associated news contents overlap at least in part, a natural solution is to aggregate the content somehow to remove duplication. Moreover, the aggregation of news provides a global view of the textual information about the specific

Proceedings of the NAACL HLT 2010: Demonstration Session, pages 5–8,
Los Angeles, California, June 2010.

location. Our system is the first available geospatial text aggregation system to our knowledge.

Within geospatial display systems, the space available to display textual information is often quite limited. We therefore need to summarize the most important and relevant information about each location, drawing from all the web pages linked to it. However, directly applying a multi-document summarization (Lin and Hovy, 2001) to the web pages will generate poor results, due to unrelated titles, duplicate articles, and noisy contents contained in web pages. When several different events have occurred at a location, more than one distinct summary may be needed. It is therefore important to deploy topic recognition (Lin and Hovy, 2000) and/or topic clustering (Osinski and Weiss, 2005) to identify and group relevant pieces of each text into single-topic 'chunks'. We develop a novel hierarchical summarization system to improve the interactivity and browsability.

3 Text Summarization

3.1 Content Extraction and Summarization

Multi-webpage summarization is different from traditional multi-doc summarization. First, most web pages are much more complex than pure text documents. Since the web contains a combination of types of information—static text, image, videos, dynamic layout, etc.—even a single page can be treated as multiple documents. Current linking functions are based on keywords, making the relevant content of each relevant web page only a limited block within the page. Second, our task is oriented to locations, and hence differs from general content summarization. Hence, we need to identify and extract the essential part(s) of the webpage linked to the geospatial imagery for summarization and display. In our work, we utilize two important features, layout and semantics, to identify and extract the relevant content.

By rendering each web page into a DOM tree, we segment the page into large blocks based on its layout, including header, footer, left bar, right bar, main block, etc. We implemented a rule-based extractor to extract the most relevant block from the web page based on the relevance to the location.

3.2 Clustering

Given a list of text blocks relevant to a local point of interest, one can employ traditional text summarization techniques to produce a short summary for each one. This solution may not be helpful, however, since a long list of pages associated with each point of interest would be very hard for users to browse. Especially when the space allocated to text display by the geospatial system is also limited, a high compression ratio is typically required for the summarization system.

The solution we adopt is to deploy cluster-based multi-document summarization. Clustering must observe two criteria: first, the location of interest, and second, the text topic. Different clustering methods can be employed. To delimit topics, a simple heuristic is to introduce as additional criterion the event/article date: when the difference in document dates within a topical cluster is (far) larger than the actual duration of the topic event, we are probably dealing with multiple separate events at the same location. Better performance is obtained by using a topic detection module first, and then clustering documents based on the topics identified.

Unfortunately, documents usually contain multiple locations and multiple topics. The problem of 'topic drift' can cause confusion in a short summary. As in (Hearst, 1997), we segment each document into several 'mini-documents', each one devoted to a single topic, and then to perform location- and topic-based clustering over the (now larger) set of mini-documents.

3.3 Hierarchical Summary Generation

Whatever the clustering approach, the result is a potentially rather large set of individual topics associated with each location. Since screen space for the summaries may be very limited next to the maps / imagery, they have to be formatted and presented for maximal interpretability. To address this problem, we adopt a hierarchical structure to display incrementally longer summaries for each location of interest. At present we have found three levels of incrementally longer summaries to be most useful.

Thumbnail: a very short 'topic' that characterizes the (clusters of) documents or segments associated with each location. We present essentially one or two single keywords -- the most informative words for each cluster. We implemented a new version of our topic signature technology, one that uses tf.idf instead of the entropy ratio, as scoring measure to rank each cluster's words.

Title: a headline-length phrase or short sentence (or two). The original titles of the web pages are often noisy or even unrelated to the current topic cluster. Sometimes, the title may be meaningless (it might for example contain the website's name "Pr Newswire"), or two different web pages may share the same title. We implemented a topic-related headline generator based on our previous work (Lin and Hovy, 2000) by incorporating a topic-based selector.

Snippet: a paragraph-length excerpt characterizing the cluster. To produce paragraph-length summaries, we implemented an extraction-based text summarizer. We built a new version of previously investigated technology (Lin and Hovy, 2001), implementing several sentence scoring techniques and a score combination function.

4 Demonstration

4.1 Geospatial Interaction

The hierarchical summarization service is built upon the geo-spatial information display system, GeoXRAY[1], a commercial product developed by Geosemble Technologies[2]. Figure 1 shows the system's display to support search and browsing of text content based on location of interest.

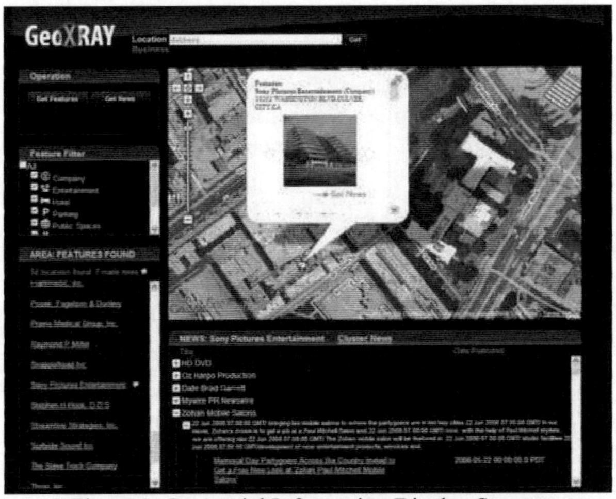

Figure 1. Geospatial Information Display System

[1]GeoXRAY: http://www.geosemble.com/products_geoxray.html
[2]Geosemble Technologies: http://www.geosemble.com/

The user can enter an address in the top search box, or search by business name. The system then centers the imagery at that address or business. Clicking on "Get Features" invokes the web services to get all features about the displayed image and displays the features in the "AREA: Features Found" list, and also draws them as points on the maps.

The user can explore the map using the navigation controller. On clicking the marker of an identified building, an information window pops up containing the associated structured web information (building name, business type, website, online images, and so on), as shown in Figure 2.

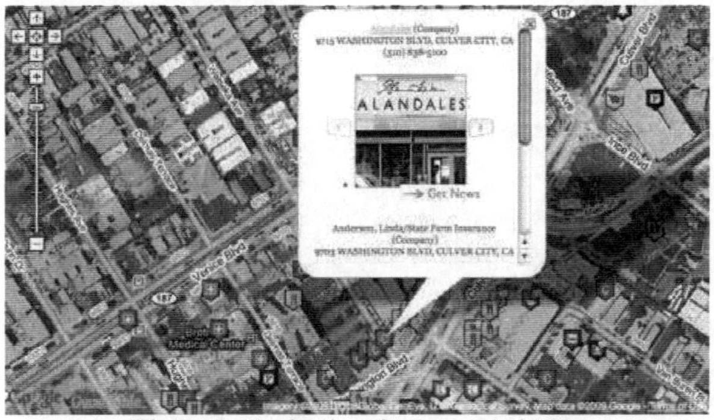

Figure 2. Navigating the Integrated Map

Clicking on "Get News" retrieves all news related to the displayed features; features with associated news show a small newspaper icon (see next to "Sony Pictures Entertainment" in Figure 4). Clicking on the icon displays the news that was linked with the feature, sorted by date.

The hierarchical summarization system, described in this paper extends the GeoXRAY system to show a summarized view of the news. The user can click on the "Cluster News" link. The results are displayed in a tree, showing the title of the cluster (thumbnail and title), under which appears a small summary of the cluster, under which appear links to all the news articles belonging to that cluster.

4.2 Summarization Example

We provide an example of our text summarization system performance in Figure 3. In this example, we have selected the location of Sony Film Studios in Culver City by clicking on the map. Figure 3(a) shows the titles and dates of some of the 126 news articles that contain the words "Sony Pictures Entertainment". As described above, these documents are clustered based on topics. Using our current parameter settings, 20 multi-result clusters are formed, leaving 34 results unclustered. (The size of clusters, or the number of clusters desired, can be varied by the user.) As mentioned above, each cluster is presented to the users by a minimal length thumbnail summary consisting of a few characteristic keywords; a partial list of these is shown in Figure 3(b). Figure 3(c) shows the result of selecting the cluster labeled "solar electrical system" (second from the bottom in Figure 3(b)), which contains two results. The summary contains the 5 top-ranked sentences from the two documents, presented in document order. In addition, the summary includes two hyperlinks to the two full texts for further inspection.

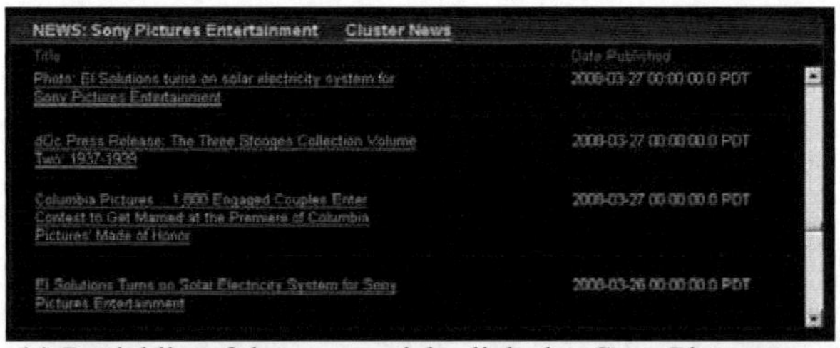

(a) Partial list of the news articles linked to Sony Pictures Entertainment

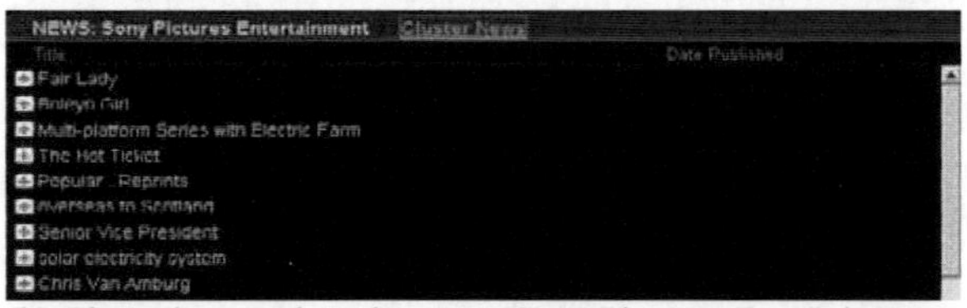

(b) Clustering results relevant to Sony Pictures Entertainment

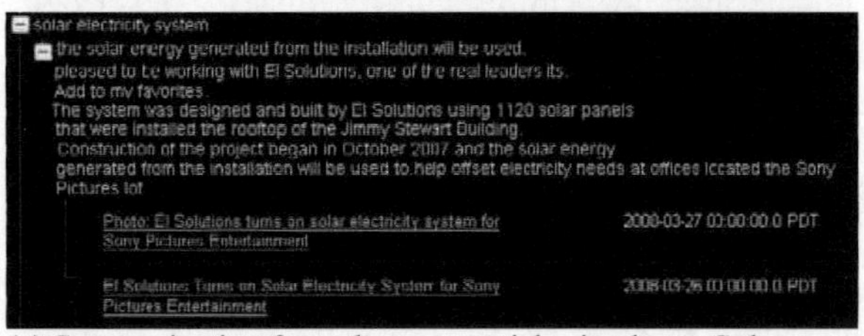

(c) Summarization from the news articles in cluster Solar electricity system

Figure 3. Document clustering and summarization for news relevant to Sony Picture Entertainment

The summary illustrates some of the strengths but also the shortcomings of the current system. It is clearly about a solar energy system installed in 2007 on top of the Jimmy Stewart Building by EI Solutions. This is enough detail for a user to determine whether or not to read the texts any further. However, two of the extracted sentences are not satisfactory: sentence 2 is broken off and sentence 3 should not be part of the news text at all. Premature sentence breaks result from inadequate punctuation and line break processing, which is still a research problem exacerbated by the complexity of web pages.

By showing the summary results, we merely demonstrate the improvement on browsability of the search system. We are relatively satisfied with the results. While the summaries are not always very good, they are uniformly understandable and completely adequate to prove that one can combine geospatial information access and text summarization in a usable and coherent manner.

Acknowledgments

Thanks to Geosemble Technologies for providing support of the geospatial information system.

References

Yih-Farn Robin Chen, Giuseppe Di Fabbrizio, David Gibbon, Serban Jora, Bernard Renger and Bin Wei. Geotracker: Geospatial and temporal rss navigation. In *WWW '07: Proceedings of the 16th International Conference on World Wide Web*, 2007.

Marti A. Hearst. TexTiling: Segmenting text into multi-paragraph subtopic passages. *Computational Linguistics*, 23(1):33–64, 1997.

Chin-Yew Lin and Eduard Hovy. The automated acquisition of topic signatures for text summarization. In *Proceedings of the 18th Conference on Computational Linguistics*, 2000.

Chin-Yew Lin and Eduard Hovy. From single to multi-document summarization: A prototype system and its evaluation. In *ACL '02: Proceedings of the 40th Annual Meeting on Association for Computational Linguistics*, 2001.

Stanislaw Osinski and Dawid Weiss. Carrot2: Design of a flexible and efficient web information retrieval framework. In *AWIC*, 2005.

Benjamin E. Teitler, Michael D. Lieberman, Daniele Panozzo, Jagan Sankaranarayanan, Hanan Samet and Jon Sperling. Newsstand: a new view on news. In *GIS '08: Proceedings of the 16th ACM SIGSPATIAL international conference on Advances in geographic information systems*, 2008.

Phrasal: A Toolkit for Statistical Machine Translation with Facilities for Extraction and Incorporation of Arbitrary Model Features

Daniel Cer, Michel Galley, Daniel Jurafsky and Christopher D. Manning
Stanford University
Stanford, CA 94305, USA

Abstract

We present a new Java-based open source toolkit for phrase-based machine translation. The key innovation provided by the toolkit is to use APIs for integrating new features (/knowledge sources) into the decoding model and for extracting feature statistics from aligned bitexts. The package includes a number of useful features written to these APIs including features for hierarchical reordering, discriminatively trained linear distortion, and syntax based language models. Other useful utilities packaged with the toolkit include: a conditional phrase extraction system that builds a phrase table just for a specific dataset; and an implementation of MERT that allows for pluggable evaluation metrics for both training and evaluation with built in support for a variety of metrics (e.g., TERp, BLEU, METEOR).

1 Motivation

Progress in machine translation (MT) depends critically on the development of new and better model features that allow translation systems to better identify and construct high quality machine translations. The popular Moses decoder (Koehn et al., 2007) was designed to allow new features to be defined using factored translation models. In such models, the individual phrases being translated can be factored into two or more abstract phrases (e.g., lemma, POS-tags) that can be translated individually and then combined in a seperate generation stage to arrive at the final target translation. While greatly enriching the space of models that can be used for phrase-based machine translation, Moses only allows features that can be defined at the level of individual words and phrases.

The Phrasal toolkit provides easy-to-use APIs for the development of arbitrary new model features. It includes an API for extracting feature statistics from aligned bitexts and for incorporating the new features into the decoding model. The system has already been used to develop a number of innovative new features (Chang et al., 2009; Galley and Manning, 2008; Galley and Manning, 2009; Green et al., 2010) and to build translation systems that have placed well at recent competitive evaluations, achieving second place for Arabic to English translation on the NIST 2009 constrained data track.[1]

We implemented the toolkit in Java because it offers a good balance between performance and developer productivity. Compared to C++, developers using Java are 30 to 200% faster, produce fewer defects, and correct defects up to 6 times faster (Phipps, 1999). While Java programs were historically much slower than similar programs written in C or C++, modern Java virtual machines (JVMs) result in Java programs being nearly as fast as C++ programs (Bruckschlegel, 2005). Java also allows for trivial code portability across different platforms.

In the remainder of the paper, we will highlight various useful capabilities, components and modeling features included in the toolkit.

2 Toolkit

The toolkit provides end-to-end support for the creation and evaluation of machine translation models. Given sentence-aligned parallel text, a new translation system can be built using a single command:

```
java edu.stanford.nlp.mt.CreateModel \
  (source.txt) (target.txt) \
  (dev.source.txt) (dev.ref) (model_name)
```

Running this command will first create word level alignments for the sentences in source.txt and target.txt using the Berkeley cross-EM aligner

[1] http://www.itl.nist.gov/iad/mig/tests/mt/2009/ResultsRelease/currentArabic.html

Proceedings of the NAACL HLT 2010: Demonstration Session, pages 9–12,
Los Angeles, California, June 2010.

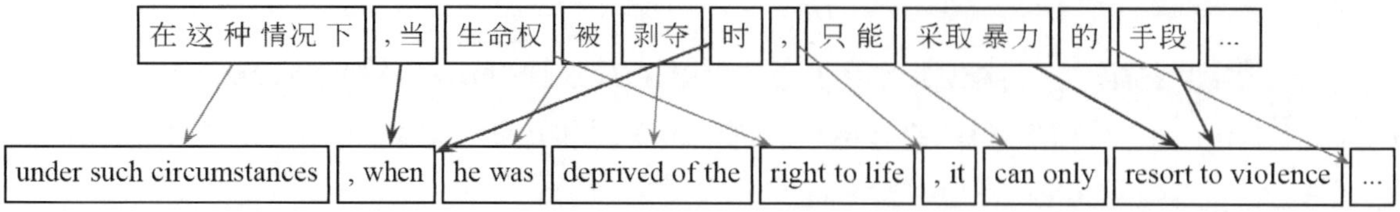

Figure 1: Chinese-to-English translation using discontinuous phrases.

(Liang et al., 2006).[2] From the word-to-word alignments, the system extracts a phrase table (Koehn et al., 2003) and hierarchical reordering model (Galley and Manning, 2008). Two n-gram language models are trained on the target.txt sentences: one over lowercased target sentences that will be used by the Phrasal decoder and one over the original source sentences that will be used for truecasing the MT output. Finally, the system trains the feature weights for the decoding model using minimum error rate training (Och, 2003) to maximize the system's BLEU score (Papineni et al., 2002) on the development data given by dev.source.txt and dev.ref. The toolkit is distributed under the GNU general public license (GPL) and can be downloaded from `http://nlp.stanford.edu/software/phrasal`.

3 Decoder

Decoding Engines The package includes two decoding engines, one that implements the left-to-right beam search algorithm that was first introduced with the Pharaoh machine translation system (Koehn, 2004), and another that provides a recently developed decoding algorithm for translating with discontinuous phrases (Galley and Manning, 2010). Both engines use features written to a common but extensible feature API, which allows features to be written once and then loaded into either engine.

Discontinuous phrases provide a mechanism for systematically translating grammatical constructions. As seen in Fig. 1, using discontinuous phrases allows us to successfully capture that the Chinese construction 当 **X** 的 can be translated as *when* **X**.

Multithreading The decoder has robust support for multithreading, allowing it to take full advantage of modern hardware that provides multiple CPU cores. As shown in Fig. 2, decoding speed scales well when the number of threads being used is increased from one to four. However, increasing the

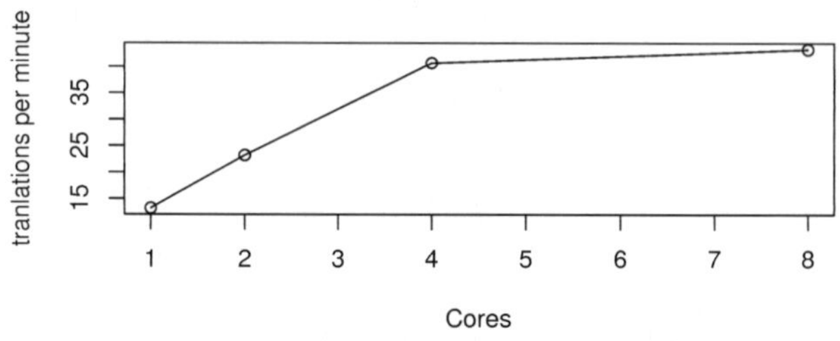

Figure 2: Multicore translations per minute on a system with two Intel Xeon L5530 processors running at 2.40GHz.

threads past four results in only marginal additional gains as the cost of managing the resources shared between the threads is starting to overwhelm the value provided by each additional thread. Moses also does not run faster with more than 4-5 threads.[3]

Feature API The feature API was designed to abstract away complex implementation details of the underlying decoding engine and provide a simple consistent framework for creating new decoding model features. During decoding, as each phrase that is translated, the system constructs a *Featurizable* object. As seen in Table 1, *Featurizable* objects specify what phrase was just translated and an overall summary of the translation being built. Code that implements a feature inspects the *Featurizable* and returns one or more named feature values. Prior to translating a new sentence, the sentence is passed to the active features for a decoding model, so that they can perform any necessary preliminary analysis.

Comparison with Moses Credible research into new features requires baseline system performance that is on par with existing state-of-the-art systems. Seen in Table 2, Phrasal meets the performance of Moses when using the exact same decoding model feature set as Moses and outperforms Moses significantly when using its own default feature set.[4]

[2] Optionally, GIZA++ (Och and Ney, 2003) can also be used to create the word-to-word alignments.

[3] `http://statmt.org/moses/?n=Moses.AdvancedFeatures (April 6, 2010)`

[4] Phrasal was originally written to replicate Moses as it was implemented in 2007 (release 2007-05-29), and the current ver-

Featurizable
Last Translated Phrase Pair
Source and Target Alignments
Partial Translation
Source Sentence
Current Source Coverage
Pointer to Prior Featurizable

Table 1: Information passed to features in the form of a *Featurizable* object for each translated phrase.

System	Features	MT06 (tune)	MT03	MT05
Moses	Moses	34.23	33.72	32.51
Phrasal	Moses	34.25	33.72	32.49
Phrasal	Default	35.02	34.98	33.21

Table 2: Comparison of two configurations of Phrasal to Moses on Chinese-to-English. One Phrasal configuration uses the standard Moses feature set for single factor phrase-based translation with distance and phrase level msd-bidirectional-fe reordering features. The other uses the default configuration of Phrasal, which replaces the phrase level msd-bidirectional-fe feature with a heirarchical reordering feature.

4 Features

The toolkit includes the basic eight phrase-based translation features available in Moses as well as Moses' implementation of lexical reordering features. In addition to the common Moses features, we also include innovative new features that improve translation quality. One of these features is a hierarchical generalization of the Moses lexical reordering model. Instead of just looking at the reordering relationship between individual phrases, the new feature examines the reordering of blocks of adjacent phrases (Galley and Manning, 2008) and improves translation quality when the material being reordered cannot be captured by single phrase. This hierarchical lexicalized reordering model is used by default in Phrasal and is responsible for the gains shown in Table 2 using the default features.

To illustrate how Phrasal can effectively be used to design rich feature sets, we present an overview of various extensions that have been built upon the Phrasal feature API. These extensions are currently not included in the release:

Target Side Dependency Language Model The n-gram language models that are traditionally used to capture the syntax of the target language do a poor job of modeling long distance syntactic relationships. For example, if there are a number of intervening words between a verb and its subject, n-gram language models will often not be of much help in selecting the verb form that agrees with the subject. The target side dependency language model feature captures these long distance relationships by providing a dependency score for the target translations produced by the decoder. This is done using an efficient quadratic time algorithm that operates within the main decoding loop rather than in a separate reranking stage (Galley and Manning, 2009).

Discriminative Distortion The standard distortion cost model used in phrase-based MT systems such as Moses has two problems. First, it does not estimate the future cost of known required moves, thus increasing search errors. Second, the model penalizes distortion linearly, even when appropriate reorderings are performed. To address these problems, we used the Phrasal feature API to design a new discriminative distortion model that predicts word movement during translation and that estimates future cost. These extensions allow us to triple the distortion limit and provide a statistically significant improvement over the baseline (Green et al., 2010).

Discriminative Reordering with Chinese Grammatical Relations During translation, a source sentence can be more accurately reordered if the system knows something about the syntactic relationship between the words in the phrases being reordered. The discriminative reordering with Chinese grammatical relations feature examines the path between words in a source-side dependency tree and uses it to evaluate the appropriateness of candidate phrase reorderings (Chang et al., 2009).

5 Other components

Training Decoding Models The package includes a comprehensive toolset for training decoding models. It supports MERT training using coordinate descent, Powell's method, line search along random search directions, and downhill Simplex. In addition to the BLEU metric, models can be trained

sion still almost exactly replicates this implementation when using only the baseline Moses features. To ensure this configuration of the decoder is still competitive, we compared it against the current Moses implementation (release 2009-04-13) and found that the performance of the two systems is still close. Tthe current Moses implementation obtains slightly lower BLEU scores, respectively 33.98 and 32.39 on MT06 and MT05.

to optimize other popular evaluation metrics such as METEOR (Lavie and Denkowski, 2009), TERp (Snover et al., 2009), mWER (Nießen et al., 2000), and PER (Tillmann et al., 1997). It is also possible to plug in other new user-created evaluation metrics.

Conditional Phrase Table Extraction Rather than first building a massive phrase table from a parallel corpus and then filtering it down to just what is needed for a specific data set, our toolkit supports the extraction of just those phrases that might be used on a given evaluation set. In doing so, it dramatically reduces the time required to build the phrase table and related data structures such as reordering models.

Feature Extraction API In order to assist in the development of new features, the toolkit provides an API for extracting feature statistics from a word-aligned parallel corpus. This API ties into the conditional phrase table extraction utility, and thus allows for the extraction of just those feature statistics that are relevant to a given data set.

6 Conclusion

Phrasal is an open source state-of-the-art Java-based machine translation system that was designed specifically for research into new decoding model features. The system supports traditional phrase-based translation as well as translation using discontinuous phrases. It includes a number of new and innovative model features in addition to those typically found in phrase-based translation systems. It is also packaged with other useful components such as tools for extracting feature statistics, building phrase tables for specific data sets, and MERT training routines that support a number of optimization techniques and evaluation metrics.

Acknowledgements

The Phrasal decoder has benefited from the helpful comments and code contributions of Pi-Chuan Chang, Spence Green, Karthik Raghunathan, Ankush Singla, and Huihsin Tseng. The software presented in this paper is based on work work was funded by the Defense Advanced Research Projects Agency through IBM. The content does not necessarily reflect the views of the U.S. Government, and no official endorsement should be inferred.

References

Thomas Bruckschlegel. 2005. Microbenchmarking C++, C#, and Java. *C/C++ Users Journal*.

P. Chang, H. Tseng, D. Jurafsky, and C.D. Manning. 2009. Discriminative reordering with Chinese grammatical relations features. In *SSST Workshop at NAACL*.

Michel Galley and Christopher D. Manning. 2008. A simple and effective hierarchical phrase reordering model. In *EMNLP*.

Michel Galley and Christopher D. Manning. 2009. Quadratic-time dependency parsing for machine translation. In *ACL*.

Michel Galley and Christopher Manning. 2010. Improving phrase-based machine translation with discontiguous phrases. In *NAACL*.

Spence Green, Michel Galley, and Christopher D. Manning. 2010. Improved models of distortion cost for statistical machine translation. In *In NAACL*.

Philipp Koehn, Franz Och, and Daniel Marcu. 2003. Statistical phrase-based translation. In *NAACL*.

P. Koehn, H. Hoang, A. Birch, C. Callison-Burch, M. Federico, N. Bertoldi, B. Cowan, W. Shen, C. Moran, R. Zens, C. Dyer, O. Bojar, A. Constantin, and E. Herbst. 2007. Moses: Open source toolkit for statistical machine translation. In *ACL*.

Philipp Koehn. 2004. Pharaoh: A beam search decoder for phrase-based statistical machine translation models. In *AMTA*.

Alon Lavie and Michael J. Denkowski. 2009. The METEOR metric for automatic evaluation of machine translation. *Machine Translation*, 23.

Percy Liang, Ben Taskar, and Dan Klein. 2006. Alignment by agreement. In *NAACL*.

Sonja Nießen, Franz Josef Och, and Hermann Ney. 2000. An evaluation tool for machine translation: Fast evaluation for MT research. In *LREC*.

Franz Josef Och and Hermann Ney. 2003. A systematic comparison of various statistical alignment models. *Computational Linguistics*, 29(1):19–51.

Franz Josef Och. 2003. Minimum error rate training in statistical machine translation. In *ACL*.

Kishore Papineni, Salim Roukos, Todd Ward, and Wei-Jing Zhu. 2002. BLEU: a method for automatic evaluation of machine translation. In *ACL*.

Geoffrey Phipps. 1999. Comparing observed bug and productivity rates for java and C++. *Softw. Pract. Exper.*, 29(4):345–358.

M. Snover, N. Madnani, B.J. Dorr, and R. Schwartz. 2009. Fluency, adequacy, or HTER?: exploring different human judgments with a tunable MT metric. In *SMT workshop at EACL*.

C. Tillmann, S. Vogel, H. Ney, A. Zubiaga, and H. Sawaf. 1997. Accelerated DP based search for statistical translation. In *In Eurospeech*.

Multilingual Propbank Annotation Tools: Cornerstone and Jubilee

Jinho D. Choi, Claire Bonial, Martha Palmer

University of Colorado at Boulder, USA
{choijd;bonial;mpalmer}@colorado.edu

Abstract

This paper demonstrates two annotation tools related to Propbank: Cornerstone and Jubilee. Propbank is a corpus in which the arguments of each verb predicate are annotated with their semantic roles. Propbank annotation also requires the choice of a sense ID for each predicate, defined in the corresponding frameset file. Jubilee expedites the annotation process by displaying several resources of syntactic and semantic information simultaneously; easy access to each of these resources allows the annotator to quickly absorb and apply the necessary syntactic and semantic information pertinent to each predicate for consistent and efficient annotation. Cornerstone is a user-friendly XML editor, customized to allow frame authors to create and edit frameset files. Both tools have been successfully adapted to many Propbank projects; they run platform independently, are light enough to run as X11 applications and support multiple languages such as Arabic, Chinese, English, Hindi and Korean.

1 Introduction

Propbank is a corpus in which the arguments of each verb predicate are annotated with their semantic roles (Palmer et al., 2005). Propbank annotation also requires the choice of a sense ID for each predicate. Thus, for each predicate in the Propbank, there exists a corresponding frameset file encompassing one or more senses of the predicate. All frameset files are written in XML, which is somewhat difficult to read and edit. Although there already exist many XML editors, most of them require some degree of knowledge of XML, and none of them are specifically customized for frameset files. This motivated the development of our own frameset editor, Cornerstone.

Jubilee is a Propbank instance editor. For each verb predicate, we create a Propbank instance that consists of the predicate's sense ID and its arguments labeled with semantic roles. Previously the allocation of tasks, the annotation of argument labels and the frameset tagging were all done as separate tasks. With Jubilee, the entire annotation procedure can be done using one tool that simultaneously provides rich syntactic information as well as comprehensive semantic information.

Both Cornerstone and Jubilee are developed in Java (JDK 6.0), so they run on any platform where the Java virtual machine is installed. They are light enough to run as X11 applications. This aspect is important because Propbank data are usually stored in a server, so annotators need to update them remotely (via SSH). One of the biggest advantages of using these tools is that they accommodate several languages; in fact, the tools have been used for Propbank projects in Arabic (M.Diab et al., 2008), Chinese (Xue and Palmer, 2009), English (Palmer et al., 2005) and Hindi, and have been tested in Korean (Han et al., 2002).

This demo paper details how to create Propbank framesets in Cornerstone, and how to annotate Propbank instances using Jubilee. There are two modes in which to run Cornerstone: multi-lemma and uni-lemma mode. In multi-lemma mode, a predicate can have multiple lem-

Proceedings of the NAACL HLT 2010: Demonstration Session, pages 13–16,
Los Angeles, California, June 2010.

mas, whereas a predicate can have only one lemma in uni-lemma mode. Jubilee also has two modes: normal and gold mode. In normal mode, annotators are allowed to view and edit only tasks that have been claimed by themselves or by one other annotator. In gold mode, adjudicators are allowed to view and edit all tasks that have undergone at least single-annotation.

2 How to obtain the tools

Cornerstone and Jubilee are available as an open source project on Google code.[1] The webpage gives detailed instructions of how to download, install and launch the tools (Choi et al., 2009a; Choi et al., 2009b).

3 Description of Cornerstone

3.1 Multi-lemma mode

Languages such as English and Hindi are expected to run in *multi-lemma* mode, due to the nature of their verb predicates. In multi-lemma mode, a predicate can have multiple lemmas (e.g., 'run', 'run out', 'run up'). The XML structure of the frameset files for such langauges is defined in a DTD file, `frameset.dtd`.

Figure 1 shows what appears when you open a frameset file, `run.xml`, in multi-lemma mode. The window consists of four panes: the frameset pane, predicate pane, roleset pane and roles pane. The frameset pane contains a frameset note reserved for information that pertains to all predicate lemmas and rolesets within the frameset file. The predicate pane contains one or more tabs titled by predicate lemmas that may include verb particle constructions. The roleset pane contains tabs titled by roleset IDs (e.g., *run*.01, *run*.02, corresponding to different senses of the predicate) for the currently selected predicate lemma (e.g., 'run'). The roles pane includes one or more roles, which represent arguments that the predicate requires or commonly takes in usage.

3.2 Uni-lemma mode

Languages such as Arabic and Chinese are expected to run in *uni-lemma* mode. Unlike multi-

[1]`http://code.google.com/p/propbank/`

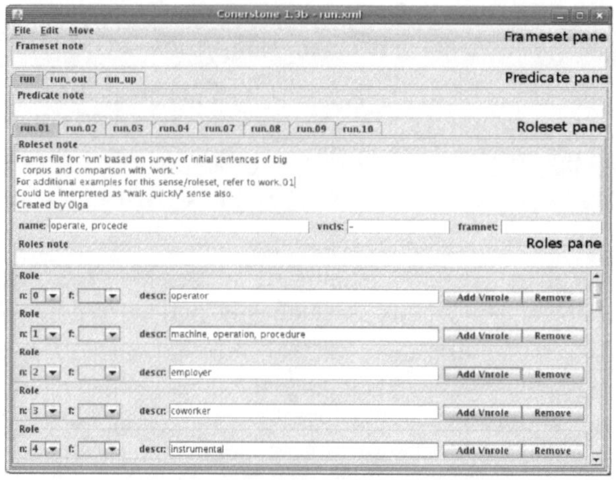

Figure 1: Open `run.xml` in multi-lemma mode

lemma mode, which allows a predicate to have multiple lemmas, uni-lemma mode allows only one lemma for a predicate. The XML structure of the frameset files for such langauges is defined in a DTD file, `verb.dtd`.

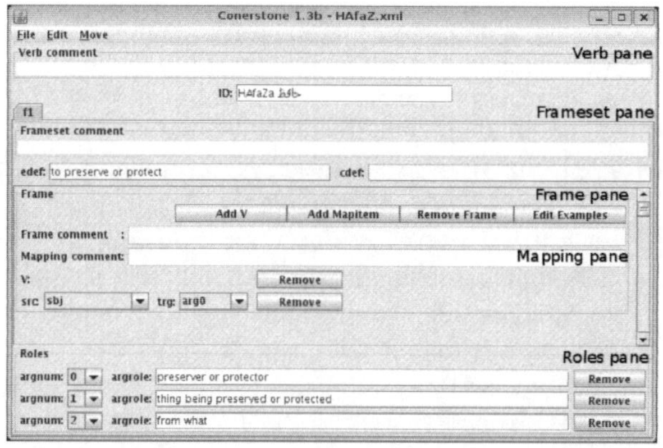

Figure 2: Open `HAfaZ.xml` in uni-lemma mode

Figure 2 shows what appears when you open a frameset file, `HAfaZ.xml`, in uni-lemma mode. The window consists of four panes: the verb pane, frameset pane, frame pane and roles pane. The verb pane contains a verb comment field for information helpful to annotators about the verb, as well as the attribute field, `ID`, which indicates the predicate lemma of the verb, represented either in the Roman alphabet or characters in other languages. The frameset pane contains several tabs titled by frameset IDs (corresponding to verb senses) for the predicate. The frame pane contains a frame comment for optional information about the frame and the mapping pane, which includes mappings between syntactic constituents and semantic arguments. The roles pane consists of a set of arguments that the predicate requires or commonly takes.

4 Description of Jubilee

4.1 Normal mode

Annotators are expected to run Jubilee in normal mode. In normal mode, annotators are allowed to view and edit only tasks claimed by themselves or one other annotator when the max-number of annotators allowed is two. Jubilee gives the option of assigning a different max-number of annotators as well.

When you run Jubilee in normal mode, you will see an open-dialog (Figure 3). There are three components in the open-dialog. The combo-box at the top shows a list of all Propbank projects. Once you select a project (e.g., `english.sample`), both `[New Tasks]` and `[My Tasks]` will be updated. `[New Task]` shows a list of tasks that have either not been claimed, or claimed by only one other annotator. `[My Tasks]` shows a list of tasks that have been claimed by the current annotator.

Figure 3: Open-dialog

Once you choose a task and click the `[Enter]` button, Jubilee's main window will be prompted (Figure 4). There are three views available in the main window: the treebank view, frameset view and argument view. By default, the treebank view shows the first tree (in the Penn Treebank format (Marcus et al., 1993)) in the selected task. The frameset view displays rolesets and allows the annotator to choose the sense of the predicate with respect to the current tree. The argument view contains buttons representing each of the Propbank argument labels.

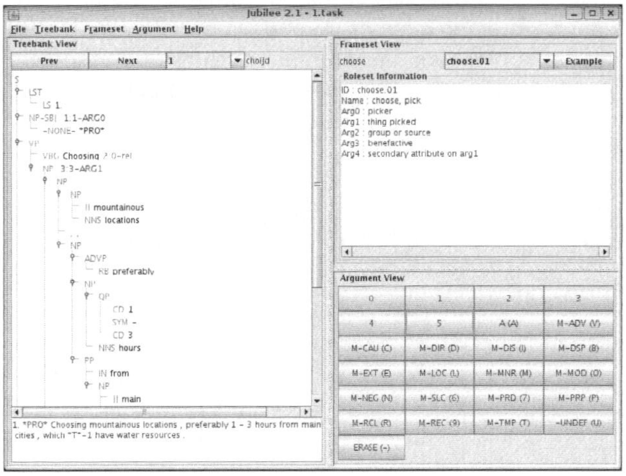

Figure 4: Jubilee's main window

4.2 Gold mode

Adjudicators are expected to run Jubilee in gold mode. In gold mode, adjudicators are allowed to view and edit all tasks that have undergone at least single-annotation. When you run Jubilee in gold mode, you will see the same open-dialog as you saw in Figure. 3. The `[New Tasks]` shows a list of tasks that have not been adjudicated, and the `[My Tasks]` shows a list of tasks that have been adjudicated. Gold mode does not allow adjudicators to open tasks that have not been at least single-annotated.

5 Demonstrations

5.1 Cornerstone

We will begin by demonstrating how to view frameset files in both multi-lemma and uni-lemma mode. In each mode, we will open an existing frameset file, compare its interface with the actual XML file, and show how intuitive it is to interact with the tool. Next, we will demonstrate how to create and edit a new frameset file either from scratch or using an existing frameset file. This demonstration will reflect several advantages of using the tool. First, the XML structure is completely transparent to the frame authors, so that no knowledge of XML is required to manage the frameset files. Second, the tool automates some of the routine work for the frame authors (e.g., assigning a new roleset/frameset ID) and gives lists of options to be chosen (e.g., a list of function tags) so that frameset creation, and the entire annotation procedure in turn, become much faster. Third, the tool checks for the completion of required fields and formatting errors so that frame authors do not have to check them manually. Finally, the tool automatically saves the changes so the work is never lost.

5.2 Jubilee

For the treebank view, we will compare Jubilee's graphical representation of the trees with the parenthetical representation of former tools: the clear visual representation of the phrase structure helps the annotator to better understand the syntax of the instance and to annotate the appropriate node within the correct span. For the frameset view, we will detail what kind of semantic information it provides as you choose different rolesets. This will highlight how Jubilee's support of roleset ID annotation not only speeds up the annotation process, but also ensures consistent annotation because the roleset information provides a guideline for the correct annotation of a particular verb sense. For the argument view, we will illustrate how to annotate Propbank arguments and use the operators for concatenations and links; thereby also demonstrating that having each of these labels clearly visible helps the annotator to remember and evaluate the appropriateness of each possible argument label. Finally, we will show how intuitive it is to adjudicate the annotations in gold mode.

6 Future work

Both Cornerstone and Jubilee have been successfully adapted to Propbank projects in several universities such as Brandeis University, the University of Colorado at Boulder, and the University of Illinois at Urbana-Champaign. We will continuously develop the tools by improving their functionalities through user-testing and feedback, and also by applying them to more languages.

Acknowledgments

Special thanks are due to Prof. Nianwen Xue of Brandeis University for his very helpful insights as well as Scott Cotton, the developer of RATS and Tom Morton, the developer of WordFreak, both previously used for PropBank annotation. We gratefully acknowledge the support of the National Science Foundation Grants CISE-CRI-0551615, Towards a Comprehensive Linguistic Annotation and CISE-CRI 0709167, Collaborative: A Multi-Representational and Multi-Layered Treebank for Hindi/Urdu, and a grant from the Defense Advanced Research Projects Agency (DARPA/IPTO) under the GALE program, DARPA/CMO Contract No. HR0011-06-C-0022, subcontract from BBN, Inc. Any opinions, findings, and conclusions or recommendations expressed in this material are those of the authors and do not necessarily reflect the views of the National Science Foundation.

References

Jinho D. Choi, Claire Bonial, and Martha Palmer. 2009a. Cornerstone: Propbank frameset editor guideline (version 1.3). Technical report, Institute of Cognitive Science, the University of Colorado at Boulder.

Jinho D. Choi, Claire Bonial, and Martha Palmer. 2009b. Jubilee: Propbank instance editor guideline (version 2.1). Technical report, Institute of Cognitive Science, the University of Colorado at Boulder.

C. Han, N. Han, E. Ko, and M. Palmer. 2002. Korean treebank: Development and evaluation. In *Proceedings of the 3rd International Conference on Language Resources and Evaluation.*

Mitchell P. Marcus, Mary Ann Marcinkiewicz, and Beatrice Santorini. 1993. Building a large annotated corpus of english: The penn treebank. *Computational Linguistics*, 19(2):313–330.

M.Diab, A.Mansouri, M.Palmer, O.Babko-Malaya, W Zaghouani, A.Bies, and M.Maamouri. 2008. A pilot arabic propbank. In *Proceedings of the 7th International Conference on Language Resources and Evaluation.*

Martha Palmer, Daniel Gildea, and Paul Kingsbury. 2005. The proposition bank: An annotated corpus of semantic roles. *Computational Linguistics*, 31(1):71–106.

Nianwen Xue and Martha Palmer. 2009. Adding semantic roles to the chinese treebank. *Natural Language Engineering*, 15(1):143–172.

KSC-PaL: A Peer Learning Agent that Encourages Students to take the Initiative*

Cynthia Kersey
Lewis University
Romeoville, IL 60446 USA
kerseycy@lewisu.edu

Barbara Di Eugenio
University of Illinois at Chicago
Chicago, IL 60607 USA
bdieugen@cs.uic.edu

Pamela Jordan and Sandra Katz
University of Pittsburgh
Pittsburgh, PA 15260 USA
pjordan+@pitt.edu
katz+@pitt.edu

Abstract

We present an innovative application of dialogue processing concepts to educational technology. In a previous corpus analysis of peer learning dialogues, we found that initiative and initiative shifts are indicative of learning, and of learning-conducive episodes. We have incorporated this finding in KSC-PaL, a peer learning agent. KSC-PaL promotes learning by encouraging shifts in task initiative.

1 Introduction

Collaborative learning has been shown to be an effective mode of learning for potentially all participants (Brown and Palincsar, 1989; Fisher, 1993; Tin, 2003). While collaboration in dialogue has long been researched in computational linguistics (Chu-Carroll and Carberry, 1998; Constantino-González and Suthers, 2000; Jordan and Di Eugenio, 1997; Soller, 2004), the study of peer learning from a computational perspective is still in the early stages.

Previous research has suggested several mechanisms that explain why peer learning is effective. Among them are: self-directed explaining (Chi et al., 1994), other-directed explaining (Ploetzner et al., 1999; Roscoe and Chi, 2007) and Knowledge Co-construction – KCC for short (Hausmann et al., 2004). KCC episodes are defined as portions of the dialogue in which students are jointly constructing a shared meaning of a concept required for problem solving. This last mechanism is the most interesting from a peer learning perspective because it is a truly collaborative construct and also because it is consistent with the widely accepted constructivist view of learning.

In our previous work (Kersey et al., 2009) we derived a model of peer interactions that operationalizes KCC via the notion of initiative shifts in dialogue. This model was based on an extensive corpus analysis in which we found a strong relationship between initiative shifts and KCC episodes. A paired t-test showed that there were significantly more initiative shifts in the annotated KCC episodes compared with the rest of the dialogue ($t(57) = 3.32$, $p = 0.0016$). The moderate effect difference between the two groups (effect size = 0.49) shows that there is a meaningful increase in the number of initiative shifts in KCC episodes compared with problem solving activity outside of the KCC episodes. Additionally, we found moderate correlations of learning with both KCC ($R^2 = 0.14$, $p = 0.02$) and with initiative shifts ($R^2 = 0.20$, $p = 0.00$).

We have incorporated this model in an innovative peer learning agent, KSC-PaL, that is designed to collaborate with a student to solve problems in the domain of computer science data structures.

2 KSC-PaL

KSC-PaL, has at its core the TuTalk System (Jordan et al., 2007), a dialogue management system that supports natural language dialogue in educational applications. In developing KSC-PaL we extended TuTalk in three ways.

The first extension is a user interface (see Figure 1) which manages communication between TuTalk and the student. Students interact with KSC-

*This work is funded by NSF grants 0536968 and 0536959.

Proceedings of the NAACL HLT 2010: Demonstration Session, pages 17–20,
Los Angeles, California, June 2010. ©2010 Association for Computational Linguistics

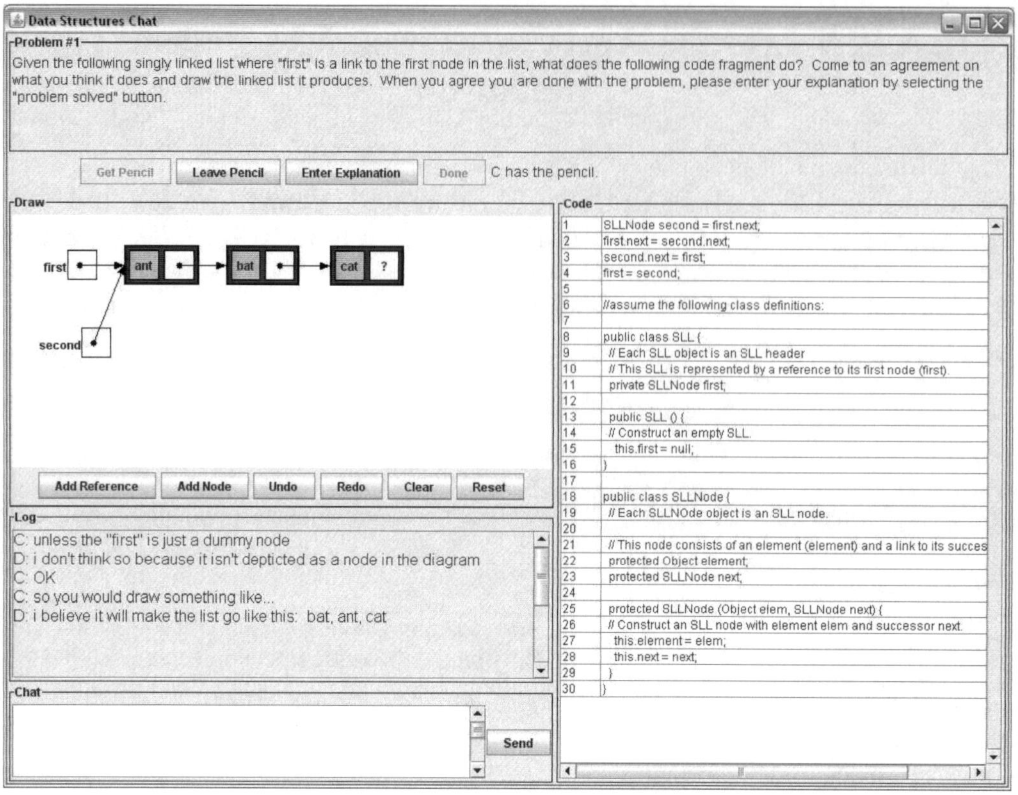

Figure 1: The KSC-PaL interface

PaL using natural language and graphical actions. The student input is processed by the interface and its related modules into an appropriate format and passed to TuTalk. Since TuTalk's interpretation module is not able to appropriately handle all student utterances, a human interpreter assists in this process. The interpreter receives a student utterance along with a list of possible matching concepts from TuTalk (see Figure 4). The interpreter then selects the most likely matching concepts from TuTalk thus assisting in natural language interpretation. If the student utterance doesn't match any of these concepts, a second list of concepts, containing student initiative utterances, are presented to the interpreter. If none of these match then all known concepts are presented to the interpreter for matching. Note that the interpreter has a limited, predetermined set of choices, corresponding to the concepts that TuTalk is aware of. In this way, his/her intervention is circumscribed.

The second addition is the incorporation of a student model that allows the KSC-PaL to track the current state of problem solving and the student's knowledge in order to guide its behavior. TuTalk's student model was replaced with one that incorporates problem solution graphs (Conati et al., 2002). Solution graphs are Bayesian networks where each node represents either an action required to solve the problem or a concept required as part of problem solving. A user's utterances and actions are then matched to these nodes. This provides KSC-PaL with information related to the student's knowledge of problem solving concepts as well as the current topic under discussion.

Thirdly, a planning module was added to TuTalk to make decisions on implementation of problem solving goals and responses to student initiative in order to manage shifts in initiative. The planning module includes an initiative tracker that codes turns with with either student initiative or agent initiative using one classifier for natural language utterances and a separate classifier for drawing and coding actions. Once a turn is classified, it is determined whether a shift in initiative has occurred by comparing the current classification with the classification of the previous turn. An average level of initiative shifts is then computed by dividing the number of initiative shifts by the total number of turns. Based on the initiative level, KSC-PaL encourages initiative shifts by using prompts, hedging, requesting feedback from the student and encouraging student criticism by intentionally making errors in problem solving.

Our evaluation of KSC-PaL (Kersey et al., June 2010) found that students learned using the agent and that KSC-PaL was was successful in encouraging shifts in initiative.

3 Demonstration Outline

We will demonstrate a problem solving episode with KSC-PaL where a user will interact with the agent as a student. Specifically we will show how KSC-PaL attempts to manage the level of initiative and how KSC-PaL reacts to student initiative.

```
1.  Amy: hi there, are you ready
      to start?
2.  Mary: sure
3.  Amy: where to begin?
4.  Mary: i don't know
5.  Amy: maybe we should draw this
6.  Amy: do you want to draw it?
7.  Mary: ok
8.  Amy: so, line 1 ...
9.  Mary: how's that?
10. Amy: hmmm
11. Amy: line 2: first.next=
      second.next
(Mary diagrams the code segment)
12. Mary: there i finished it
13. Amy: looks good
14. Amy: i think we're done drawing
15. Mary: yes
16. Amy: basically, it switches the
     first and second elements
17. Mary: right
18. Amy: ill write the explanation
19. Mary: ok
```

Figure 2: Problem Solving Example

Figure 2 shows an excerpt from a typical problem solving session. Amy, the agent, attempts to maintain a balanced level of initiative either by encouraging the student (Mary) to take initiative, or by taking initiative. In lines 10 and 11, the agent uses a prompt followed by repetition of the problem solving goal to encourage the student to retain the initiative. However, in line 16 the agent takes initiative by proposing a solution to the problem.

KSC-PaL is also able to manage the situation where the student takes initiative in the dialogue in an unanticipated manner, as shown in Figure 3. In line 3, Mary asks a question that is not expected at this point in the problem solving process and the agent responds appropriately in line 4. KSC-PaL is able to respond to a set of student initiations derived from corpus data, such as the one in this excerpt. Additionally, the agent responds in a generic manner to other unanticipated initiations and directs the student back to problem solving.

```
1.  Mary: let's look at the code
2.  Amy: so, i think first and
      second both equal bat
3.  Mary: is second a reference or
      a node?
4.  Amy: second is a reference
```

Figure 3: Student Initiative Example

References

A. L. Brown and A. S. Palincsar, 1989. *Guided, cooperative learning and individual knowledge acquisition*, pages 307–226. Lawrence Erlbaum Associates, Hillsdale, NJ.

M.T.H. Chi, N. De Leeuw, M.H. Chiu, and C. LaVancher. 1994. Eliciting self-explanations improves understanding. *Cognitive Science*, 18(3):439–477.

Jennifer Chu-Carroll and Sandra Carberry. 1998. Collaborative response generation in planning dialogues. *Computational Linguistics*, 24(3):355–400.

Cristina Conati, Abigail Gertner, and Kurt VanLehn. 2002. Using Bayesian networks to manage uncertainty in student modeling. *User Modeling and User-Adapted Interaction*, 12(4):371–417.

María de los Angeles Constantino-González and Daniel D. Suthers. 2000. A coached collaborative learning environment for entity-relationship modeling. *Intelligent Tutoring Systems*, pages 324–333.

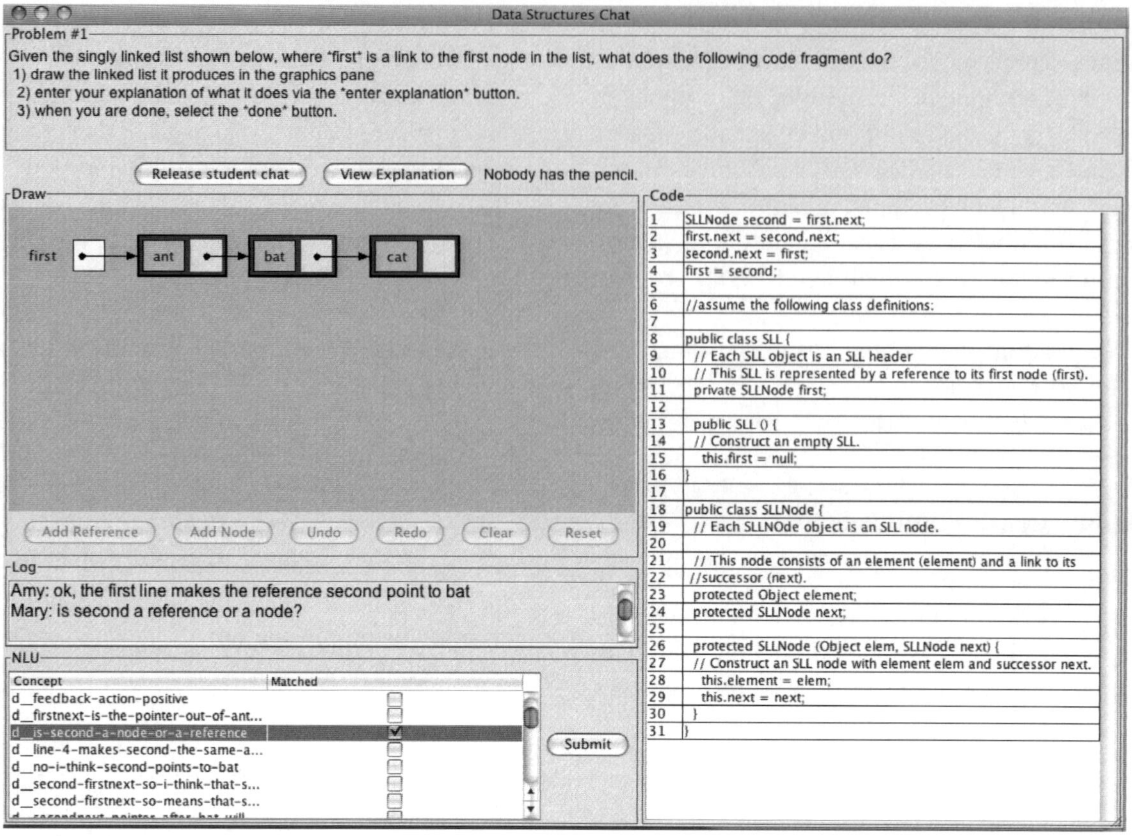

Figure 4: The interface for the human interpreter

E. Fisher. 1993. Distinctive features of pupil-pupil classroom talk and their relationship to learning: How discursive exploration might be encouraged. *Language and Education*, 7:239–257.

Robert G.M. Hausmann, Michelene T.H. Chi, and Marguerite Roy. 2004. Learning from collaborative problem solving: An analysis of three hypothesized mechanisms. In K.D Forbus, D. Gentner, and T. Regier, editors, *26th Annual Conference of the Cognitive Science Society*, pages 547–552, Mahwah, NJ.

Pamela W. Jordan and Barbara Di Eugenio. 1997. Control and initiative in collaborative problem solving dialogues. In *Working Notes of the AAAI Spring Symposium on Computational Models for Mixed Initiative*, pages 81–84, Menlo Park, CA.

Pamela W Jordan, Brian Hall, Michael A. Ringenberg, Yui Cue, and Carolyn Penstein Rosé. 2007. Tools for authoring a dialogue agent that participates in learning studies. In *Artificial Intelligence in Education, AIED 2007*, pages 43–50.

Cynthia Kersey, Barbara Di Eugenio, Pamela Jordan, and Sandra Katz. 2009. KSC-PaL: a peer learning agent that encourages students to take the initiative. In *Proceedings of the Fourth Workshop on Innovative Use of NLP for Building Educational Applications*, pages 55–63. Association for Computational Linguistics.

Cynthia Kersey, Barbara Di Eugenio, Pamela Jordan, and Sandra Katz. June 2010. KSC-PaL: A peer learning agent. In *ITS 2010, The 10th International Conference on Intelligent Tutoring Systems*, Pittsburgh, PA.

R. Ploetzner, P. Dillenbourg, M. Preier, and D. Traum. 1999. Learning by explaining to oneself and to others. *Collaborative learning: Cognitive and computational approaches*, pages 103–121.

Rod D. Roscoe and Michelene T. H. Chi. 2007. Understanding tutor learning: Knowledge-building and knowledge-telling in peer tutors' explanations and questions. *Review of Educational Research*, 77(4):534–574.

Amy Soller. 2004. Computational modeling and analysis of knowledge sharing in collaborative distance learning. *User Modeling and User-Adapted Interaction*, Volume 14(4):351–381, January.

Tan Bee Tin. 2003. Does talking with peers help learning? the role of expertise and talk in convergent group discussion tasks. *Journal of English for Academic Purposes*, 2(1):53–66.

A Detailed, Accurate, Extensive, Available English Lexical Database

Adam Kilgarriff
Lexical Computing Ltd
Brighton, UK
adam@lexmasterclass.com

Abstract

We present an English lexical database which is fuller, more accurate and more consistent than any other. We believe this to be so because the project has been well-planned, with a 12-month intensive planning phase prior to the lexicography beginning; well-resourced, employing a team of fifteen highly experienced lexicographers for a thirty-month main phase; it has had access to the latest corpus and dictionary-editing technology; it has not been constrained to meet any goals other than an accurate description of the language; and it has been led by a team with singular experience in delivering high-quality and innovative resources. The lexicon will be complete in Summer 2010 and will be available for NLP groups, on terms designed to encourage its research use.

1 Introduction

Most NLP applications need lexicons. NLP researchers have used databases from dictionary publishers (Boguraev and Briscoe, 1989; Wilks et al., 1996), or developed NLP resources (COMLEX (Macleod et al., 1994), XTAG (Doran et al., 1994)) or used WordNet,(Fellbaum, 1998) or have switched to fully corpus-based strategies which need no lexicons. However the publishers' dictionaries were pre-corpus, often inconsistent, and licencing constraints were in the end fatal. COMLEX and XTAG address only syntax; WordNet, only semantics. Also these resources were not produced by experienced lexicographers, nor according to a detailed, stringent 'style guide' specifying how to handle all the phenomena (in orthography, morphology, syntax, semantics and pragmatics, from spelling variation to register to collocation to sense distinction) that make lexicography complex. Unsupervised corpus methods are intellectually exciting but do not provide the lexical facts that many applications need.

We present DANTE (Database of Analysed Texts of English), an English lexical database. For the commonest 50,000 words of English, it gives a detailed account of the word's meaning(s), grammar, phraseology and collocation and any noteworthy facts about its pragmatics or distribution.

In outline this is what dictionaries have been doing for many years. This database is of more interest to NLP than others (for English) because of its:

- quality and consistency
- level of detail
- number of examples
- accountability to the corpus
- purity: it has been created only as an analysis of English, and has not been compromised by publishing constraints or other non-lexicographic goals
- availability, on licencing terms that promote its research use and also the re-use of enhanced versions created by NLP groups.

2 The Project

The overall project is the preparation of a New English Irish Dictionary, and is funded by Foras na Gaeilge, the official body for the (Gaelic) Irish language.[1] The project was designed according to a

[1] FnG was set up following the Good Friday Agreement of 1998 on Northern Ireland, between the Governments of the Re-

Proceedings of the NAACL HLT 2010: Demonstration Session, pages 21–24,
Los Angeles, California, June 2010.

model where the first stage of the production of a blingual dictionary is a target-language-neutral monolingual analysis of the source language listing all the phenomena that might possibly have an unexpected translation. (The next stages are then translation and 'finishing'.) The 2.3 MEuro contract for the analysis of English was won by Lexicography MasterClass Ltd in 2007.[2] The lexicographers are working on the letter 's' at time of writing and the database will be complete in Summer 2010.

3 Lexicography

Writing a dictionary is a large and complex undertaking. Planning is paramount.

In the planning phase, we identified all the aspects of the behaviour of English words which a full account of the lexicon should cover. We then found words exemplifying all aspects, and prepared a sample of one hundred model entries, where the hundred words chosen covered all the principal phenomena (Atkins and Grundy, 2006). A detailed style guide and corresponding DTD were written. We created the New Corpus for Ireland (NCI) (Kilgarriff, 2006), and set up a corpus query system (Lexical Computing's Sketch Engine; http://www.sketchengine.co.uk) and dictionary editing system (IDM's DPS: http://www.idm.fr) for the project to use. 50,000 headwords were identified and each was classified into one of eighteen categories according to type and complexity. This supported detailed planning of lexicographers' workloads and hence, scheduling, as well as adding to the richness of the data. Template entries (Atkins and Rundell, 2008, pp123-128) were developed for 68 lexical sets and for words belonging to these sets, the template was automatically inserted into the draft dictionary, saving lexicographer time and encouraging consistency.

We identified forty syntactic patterns for verbs, eighteen for nouns and eighteen for adjectives. Lexicographers were required to note all the patterns that applied for each word sense.

The lexicographers were all known to the management team beforehand for their high-quality work. They were trained in the dictionary style at two workshops, and their work was thoroughly checked throughout the project, with failings reported back and progress monitored.

A typical short entry is *honeymoon* (shown here in full but for truncated examples). Note the level of detail including senses, subsenses, grammatical structures and collocations. All points are exemplified by one or usually more corpus example sentences. (The style guide, available online, states the conditions for giving one, two or three examples for a phenomenon.)

honeymoon
- *n* holiday after wedding
  Following the wedding day, Jane and ...
  Upon your return from **honeymoon** ...
  Lee and Zoe left for a **honeymoon** *in ...*
  SUPPORT VERB spend
    They now live in Cumbernauld after spending ...
    Their **honeymoon** *was spent at Sandals ...*
  SUPPORT VERB have
    I hope that you have an absolutely fantastic ...
    The reception was held at the local pub and ...
  SUPPORT PREP on
    I have a ring on my left hand which Martha ...
    The groom whisked the bride off on **honeymoon** ...
    This particular portrait was a festive affair, ...
  STRUCTURE N_premod
    destination hotel suite holiday night couple
    Classic **honeymoon** *destinations like the ...*
    We can help and recommend all types of ...
    We were staying in the **honeymoon** *suite ...*
    A magical **honeymoon** *holiday in the beautiful ...*
    Our honeymoon packages offer a wide range of ...
    It is the favourite of our many **honeymoon** *couples.*
- *v* spend one's honeymoon
  STRUCTURE Particle (locative)
    They'll be **honeymooning** *in Paris (ooh, la la).*
    Mr and Mrs Maunder will **honeymoon** *in ...*
    The couple spent the early part of their ...
    A Dave Lister from five years in the future is ...
- *n* period of grace
  VARIANT FORM **honeymoon period**
    Since his May 1997 landslide election, Blair has ...
    The UN and Europe were pan national organisations
  CHUNK the honeymoon is over
    VARIANT the honey moon period is over
    The shortest post-election **honeymoon** *is over.*
    Could the **honeymoon** *period be over that quickly?*

public of Ireland and the UK. FnaG is an institution of the two countries.

[2]Lexicography MasterClass had also previously undertaken the planning of the project.

4 Corpus strategy and innovation

The project team combined expertise in corpora, computational linguistics and lexicography, and from the outset the project was to be solidly corpus-based. In the planning phase we had built the NCI: by the time the compilation phase started, in 2007, it was evident not only that the NCI would no longer capture current English, but also that the field had moved on and at 250m words, it was too small. We appended the Irish English data from the NCI to the much larger and newer UKWaC (Ferraresi et al., 2008) and added some contemporary American newspaper text to create the project corpus, which was then pos-tagged with TreeTagger [3] and loaded into the Sketch Engine.

The distinctive feature of the Sketch Engine is 'word sketches': one-page, corpus-driven summaries of a word's grammatical and collocational behaviour. The corpus is parsed and a table of collocations is given for each grammatical relation. For DANTE, the set of grammatical relations was defined to give an exact match to the grammatical patterns that the lexicographers were to record. The same names were used. The word sketch for the word would, in so far as the POS-tagging, parsing, and statistics worked correctly, identify precisely the grammatical patterns and collocations that the lexicographer needed to note in the dictionary.

As is evident, a very large number of corpus sentences needed taking from the corpus into the dictionary. This was streamlined with two processes: GDEX, for sorting the examples so that the 'best' (according to a set of heuristics) are shown to the lexicographer first (Kilgarriff et al., 2008), and 'one-click-copying' of sentences onto the clipboard (including highlighting the nodeword). (In contrast to a finished dictionary, examples were not edited.)

5 XML-based dictionary preparation

The document type definition uses seventy-two elements. It is as restrictive as possible, given that accuracy and then clarity take priority. Lexicographers were not permitted to submit work which did not validate. Wherever there was a fixed range of possible values for an information field, the list was included in the DTD as possible values for an attribute and the lexicographer used menu-selection rather than text-entry.

The database was also used for checking potential problems in a number of ways. For example, there are some word senses where examples are not required, but it is unusual for both senses of a two-or-more-sense word not to need examples, so we routinely used XML searching to check lexicographers' work for any such cases and scrutinised them prior to approval.

6 None of the usual constraints

Most dictionary projects are managed by publishers who are focused on the final (usually print) product, so constraints such as fitting in limited page-space, or using simplified codes to help naive users, or responding to the marketing department, or tailoring the analysis according to the specialist interests of some likely users, or features of the target language (for a bilingual dictionary) usually play a large role in the instructions given to lexicographers. In this project, with the separation of the project team from the publisher, we were unusually free of such compromising factors.

7 Leadership

Many lexicographic projects take years or decades longer than scheduled, and suffer changes of intellectual leadership, or are buffeted by political and economic constraints, all of which produce grave inconsistencies of style, scale and quality between different sections of the data. A consistent lexicon is impossible without consistent and rigorous management. The credentials of the managers are an indicator of the likely quality of the data.

Sue Atkins, the project manager, has been the driving force behind the Collins-Robert English/French Dictionaries (first two editions), the COBUILD project (with John Sinclair), The European Association for Lexicography (with Reinhart Hartmann), the British National Corpus, the Oxford Hachette English/French dictionaries (assisted by Valerie Grundy, DANTE Chief Editor) and with Charles Fillmore, FrameNet. She has co-published the Oxford Guide to Practical Lexicography with Michael Rundell, another of the project management

[3] http://www.ims.uni-stuttgart.de/projekte/corplex/TreeTagger/

team, who has been Managing Editor of a large number of dictionaries at Longman and Macmillan.

8 Licencing

In the late 1980s it seemed likely that Longman Dictionary of Contemporary English (LDOCE) would have a great impact on NLP. But its star rose, but then promptly fell. As a Longman employee with the task of developing LDOCE use within NLP, the first author investigated the reasons long and hard.

The problem was that NLP groups could not do anything with their LDOCE-based work. They could describe the work in papers, but the work itself was embedded in enhanced versions of LDOCE, or LDOCE-derived resources, and the licence that allowed them to use LDOCE did not alow them to publish or licence or give away any such resource. So LDOCE research, for academics, was a dead end.

A high-quality dictionary represents an investment of millions so one cannot expect its owners to give it away. The challenge then is to arrive at a model for a dictionary's use in which its exploration and enhancement is encouraged, and is not a dead end, and also in which the owner's interest in a return on investment is respected.

DANTE will be made available in a way designed to meet these goals. It will be licenced for NLP research for no fee. The licence will not allow the licencee to pass on the resource, but will include an undertaking from the owner to pass on the licencee's enhanced version to other groups on the same terms (provided it passes quality tests). The owner, or its agent, will also, where possible, integrate and cross-validate enhancements from different users. The owner will retain the right to licence the enhanced data, for a fee, for commercial use. The model is presented fully in (Kilgarriff, 1998).

9 DANTE Disambiguation

'DANTE disambiguation' is a program currently in preparation which takes arbitrary text and, for each content word in the text, identifies the DANTE patterns it matches and thereby assigns it to one of the word's senses in the DANTE database. It is designed to demonstrate the potential that DANTE has for NLP, and to undertake in a systematic way a piece of work that many DANTE users would otherwise need to do themselves: converting as many DANTE data fields as possible into methods which either do or do not match a particular instance of the word. The program will be freely available alongside the database.

Acknowledgments

Thanks to colleagues on the project, particularly the management team of Sue Atkins, Michael Rundell, Valerie Grundy, Diana Rawlinson and Cathal Convery.

References

Sue Atkins and Valerie Grundy. 2006. Lexicographic profiling: an aid to consistency in dictionary entry design. In *Proc. Euralex*, Torino.

Sue Atkins and Michael Rundell. 2008. *Oxford Guide to Practical Lexicography*. OUP, Oxford.

Bran Boguraev and Ted Briscoe, editors. 1989. *Computational lexicography for natural language processing*. Longman, London.

Christy Doran, Dania Egedi, Beth Ann Hockey, B. Srinivas, and Martin Zaidel. 1994. Xtag system: a wide coverage grammar for english. In *Proc. COLING*, pages 922–928.

Christiane Fellbaum, editor. 1998. *WordNet, an electronic lexical database*. MIT Press.

Adriano Ferraresi, Eros Zanchetta, Marco Baroni, and Silvia Bernardini. 2008. Introducing and evaluating UKWaC, a very large web-derived corpus of English. In *ProcWAC4, LREC, Marrakesh*.

Adam Kilgarriff, Milos Husak, Katy McAdam, Michael Rundell, and Pavel Rychly. 2008. Gdex: Automatically finding good dictionary examples in a corpus. In *Proc. Euralex*, Barcelona.

Adam Kilgarriff. 1998. Business models for dictioanries and NLP. *Int Jnl Lexicography*, 13(2):107–118.

Adam Kilgarriff. 2006. Efficient corpus development for lexicography: building the new corpus for ireland. *Language Resources and Evaluation Journal*.

Catherine Macleod, Ralph Grishman, and Adam Meyers. 1994. The comlex syntax project: the first year. In *ProcHuman Language Technology workshop*, pages 8–12.

Yorick Wilks, Brian Slator, and Louise Guthrie. 1996. *Electric words: dictionaries, computers, and meanings*. MIT Press, Cambridge, MA, USA.

An Interactive Tool for Supporting Error Analysis for Text Mining

Elijah Mayfield
Language Technologies Institute
Carnegie Mellon University
5000 Forbes Ave
Pittsburgh, PA 15216, USA
elijah@cmu.edu

Carolyn Penstein-Rosé
Language Technologies Institute
Carnegie Mellon University
5000 Forbes Ave
Pittsburgh, PA 15216, USA
cprose@cs.cmu.edu

Abstract

This demo abstract presents an interactive tool for supporting error analysis for text mining, which is situated within the Summarization Integrated Development Environment (SIDE). This freely downloadable tool was designed based on repeated experience teaching text mining over a number of years, and has been successfully tested in that context as a tool for students to use in conjunction with machine learning projects.

1 Introduction

In the past decade, more and more work in the language technologies community has shifted from work on formal, rule-based methods to work involving some form of text categorization or text mining technology. At the same time, use of this technology has expanded; where it was once accessible only to those within studying core language technologies, it is now almost ubiquitous. Papers involving text mining can currently be found even in core social science and humanities conferences.

The authors of this demonstration are involved in regular teaching of an applied machine learning course, which attracts students from virtually every field, including a variety of computer science related fields, the humanities and social sciences, and the arts. In five years of teaching this course, what has emerged is the finding that the hardest skill to impart to students is the ability to do a good error analysis. In response to this issue, the interactive error analysis tool presented here was designed, developed, and successfully tested with students.

In the remainder of this demo abstract, we offer an overview of the development environment that provides the context for this work. We then describe on a conceptual level the error analysis process that the tool seeks to support. Next, we step through the process of conducting an error analysis with the interface. We conclude with some directions for our continued work, based on observation of students' use of this interface.

2 Overview of SIDE

The interactive error analysis interface is situated within an integrated development environment for building summarization systems. Note that the SIDE (Kang et al., 2008) software and comprehensive user's manual are freely available for download[1]. We will first discuss the design of SIDE from a theoretical standpoint, and then explore the details of practical implementation.

2.1 Design Goals

SIDE was designed with the idea that documents, whether they are logs of chat discussions, sets of posts to a discussion board, or notes taken in a course, can be considered relatively unstructured. Nevertheless, when one thinks about their interpretation of a document, or how they would use the information found within a document, then a structure emerges. For example, an argument written in a paper often begins with a thesis statement, followed by supporting points, and finally a conclusion. A reader

[1]SIDE and its documentation are downloadable from http://www.cs.cmu.edu/~cprose/SIDE.html

Proceedings of the NAACL HLT 2010: Demonstration Session, pages 25–28,
Los Angeles, California, June 2010.

can identify with this structure even if there is nothing in the layout of the text that indicates that certain sentences within the argument have a different status from the others. Subtle cues in the language can be used to identify those distinct roles that sentences might play.

Conceptually, then, the use of SIDE proceeds in two main parts. The first part is to construct filters that can impose that structure on the texts to be summarized, to identify the role a sentence is playing in a document; and the second part is constructing specifications of summaries that refer to that structure, such as subsets of extracted text or data visualizations. This demo is primarily concerned with supporting error analysis for text mining. Thus, the first of these two stages will be the primary focus.

This approach to summarization was inspired by the process described in (Teufel and Moens, 2002). That work focused on the summarization of scientific articles to describe a new work in a way which rhetorically situates that work's contribution within the context of related prior work. This is done by first overlaying structure onto the documents to be summarized, categorizing the sentences they contain into one of a number of rhetorical functions. Once this structure is imposed, using the information it provides was shown to increase the quality of generated summaries.

2.2 Building Text Mining Models with SIDE

This demo assumes the user has already interacted with the SIDE text mining interface for model building, including feature extraction and machine learning, to set up a model. Defining this in SIDE terms, to train the system and create a model, the user first has to define a filter. Filters are trained using machine learning technology. Two customization options are available to analysts in this process.

The first and possibly most important is the set of customization options that affect the design of the attribute space. The standard attribute space is set up with one attribute per unique feature - the value corresponds to the number of times that feature occurs in a text. Options include unigrams, bigrams, part-of-speech bigrams, stemming, and stopword removal.

The next step is the selection of the machine learning algorithm that will be used. Dozens of options are made available through the Weka toolkit (Witten and Frank, 2005), although some are more commonly used than others. The three options that are most recommended to analysts beginning work with machine learning are Naïve Bayes (a probabilistic model), SMO (Weka's implementation of Support Vector Machines), and J48, which is one of many Weka implementations of a Decision Tree learner. SMO is considered state-of-the-art for text classification, so we expect that analysts will frequently find that to be the best choice.

As this error analysis tool is built within SIDE, we focus on applications to text mining. However, this tool can also be used on non-text data sets, so long as they are first preprocessed through SIDE. The details of our error analysis approach are not specific to any individual task or machine learning algorithm.

3 High Level View of Error Analysis

In an insightful usage of applied machine learning, a practitioner will design an approach that takes into account what is known about the structure of the data that is being modeled. However, typically, that knowledge is incomplete, and there is thus a good chance that the decisions that are made along the way are suboptimal. When the approach is evaluated, it is possible to determine based on the proportion and types of errors whether the performance is acceptable for the application or not. If it is not, then the practitioner should engage in an error analysis process to determine what is malfunctioning and what could be done to better model the structure in the data.

In well-known machine learning toolkits such as Weka, some information is available about what errors are being made. Predictions can be printed out, to allow a researcher to identify how a document is being classified. One common format for summarizing these predictions is a confusion matrix, usually printed in a format like:

```
 a  b   <-- classified as
67 19 |  a = PT
42 70 |  b = DR
```

This lists, for example, that 19 text segments were classified as type DR but were actually type PT. While this gives a rough view of what errors are

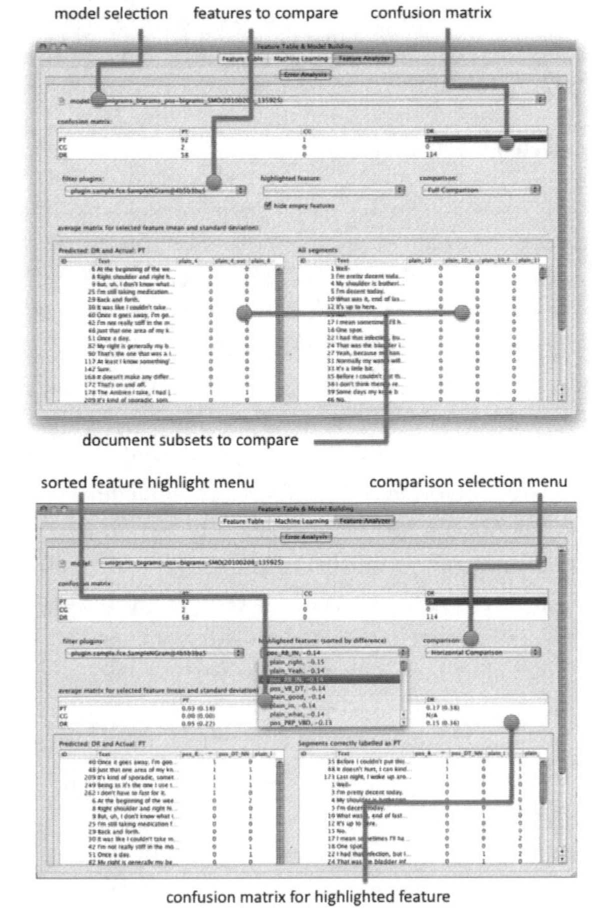

Figure 1: The error analysis interface with key functionality locations highlighted.

appearing, it gives no indication of why the errors are being made. This is where a more extensive error analysis is necessary. Two common ways to approach this question are top down, which starts with a learned model, and bottom up, which starts with the confusion matrix from that model's performance estimate. In the first case, the model is examined to find the attributes that are treated as most important. These are the attributes that have the greatest influence on the predictions made by the learned model, and thus these attributes provide a good starting point. In the second case, the bottom-up case, one first examines the confusion matrix to identify large off-diagonal cells, which represent common confusions. The error analysis for any error cell is then the process of determining relations between three sets of text segments[2] related to that cell.

Within the "classified as DR but actually PT" cell, for instance, error analysis would require finding what makes these examples most different from examples correctly classified as PT, and what makes these examples most similar to those correctly classified as DR. This can be done by identifying attributes that mostly strongly differentiate the first two sets, and attributes most similar between the first and third sets. An ideal approach would combine these two directions.

4 Error Analysis Process

Visitors to this demo will have the opportunity to experiment with the error analysis interface. It will be set up with multiple data sets and previously trained text mining models. These models can first be examined from the model building window, which contains information such as:

- Global feature collection, listing all features that were included in the trained model.
- Cross-validation statistics, including variance and kappa statistics, the confusion matrix and other general information.
- Weights or other appropriate information for the text mining model that was trained.

By moving to the error analysis interface, the user can explore a model more deeply. The first step is to select a model to examine. By default, all text segments that were evaluated in cross-validation display in a scrolling list in the bottom right corner of the window. Each row contains the text within a segment, and the associated feature vector. Users will first be asked to examine this data to understand the magnitude of the error analysis challenge.

Clicking on a cell in the confusion matrix (at the top of the screen) will fill the scrolling list at the bottom left corner of the screen with the classified segments that fall in that cell. A comparison chooser dropdown menu gives three analysis options - full, horizontal, and vertical. By default, full comparison

[2]Our interface assumes that the input text has been segmented already; depending on the task involved, these segments may correspond to a sentence, a paragraph, or even an entire document.

is selected, and shows all text segments used in training. The two additional modes of comparison allow some insight into what features are most representative of the subset of segments in that cell, compared to the correct predictions aligned with that cell (either vertically or horizontally within the confusion matrix). By switching to horizontal comparison, the scrolling list on the right changes to display only text segments that fall in the cell which is along the confusion matrix diagonal and horizontal to the selected cell. Switching to vertical comparison changes this list to display segments categorized in the cell which is along the diagonal and vertically aligned with the selected error cell.

Once a comparison method is selected, there is a feature highlighting dropdown menu which is of use. The contents in this menu are sorted by degree of difference between the segments in the two lists at the bottom of the screen. This means, for a horizontal comparison, that features at the top of this list are the most different between the two cells (this difference is displayed in the menu). We compute this difference by the difference in expected (average) value for that feature between the two sets. In a vertical comparison, features are ranked by similarity, instead of difference. Once a feature is selected from this menu, two significant changes are made. The first is that a second confusion matrix appears, giving the confusion matrix values (mean and standard deviation) for the highlighted feature. The second is that the two segment lists are sorted according to the feature being highlighted.

User interface design elements were important in this design process. One option available to users is the ability to "hide empty features," which removes features which did not occur at all in one or both of the sets being studied. This allows the user to focus on features which are most likely to be causing a significant change in a classifier's performance. It is also clear that the number of different subsets of classified segments can become very confusing, especially when comparing various types of error in one session. To combat this, the labels on the lists and menus will change to reflect some of this information. For instance, the left-hand panel gives the predicted and actual labels of the segments you have highlighted, while the right-hand panel is labelled with the name of the category of correct prediction you are comparing against. The feature highlighting dropdown menu also changes to reflect similar information about the type of comparison being made.

5 Future Directions

This error analysis tool has been used in the text mining unit for an Applied Machine Learning course with approximately 30 students. In contrast to previous semesters where the tool was not available to support error analysis, the instructor noticed that many more students were able to begin surpassing shallow observations, instead forming hypotheses about where the weaknesses in a model are, and what might be done to improve performance.

Based on our observations, however, the error analysis support could still be improved by directing users towards features that not only point to differences and similarities between different subsets of instances, but also to more information about how features are being used in the trained model. This can be implemented either in algorithm-specific ways (such as displaying the weight of features in an SVM model) or in more generalizable formats, for instance, through information gain. Investigating how to score these general aspects, and presenting this information in an intuitive way, are directions for our continued development of this tool.

Acknowledgements

This research was supported by NSF Grant DRL-0835426.

References

Moonyoung Kang, Sourish Chaudhuri, Mahesh Joshi, and Carolyn Penstein-Rosé 2008. *SIDE: The Summarization Integrated Development Environment*. Proceedings of the Association for Computational Linguistics, Demo Abstracts.

Simone Teufel and Marc Moens 2002. *Summarizing Scientific Articles: Experiments with Relevance and Rhetorical Status*. Computational Linguistics, Vol. 28, No. 1.

Ian Witten and Eibe Frank 2005. *Data Mining: Practical Machine Learning Tools and Techniques*, second edition. Elsevier: San Fransisco.

Serious Game Environments for Language and Culture Education

Alicia Sagae, W. Lewis Johnson, and Rebecca Row
Alelo, Inc.
12910 Culver Boulevard, Suite J
Los Angeles, CA 90066, USA
{asagae, ljhonson, rrow}@alelo.com

Abstract

In this demonstration we will present technologies that enable learners to engage in spoken conversations in foreign languages, integrating intelligent tutoring and serious game capabilities into a package that helps learners quickly acquire communication skills. Conversational AI technologies based on the SAIBA framework for dialog modeling are realized in this 3-D game environment. Participants will be introduced to tools for authoring dialogs in this framework, and will have an opportunity to experience learning with Alelo products, including the Operational Language and Culture Training System (OLCTS).

1 Introduction

Alelo's language and culture education environments, including The Tactical Language and Culture Training System (TLCTS) and the Operational Language and Culture Training System (OLCTS), are AI-enhanced learning platforms that help learners quickly acquire communication skills in foreign languages and cultures. They have been developed by Alelo, Inc. based on a prototype developed at the University of Southern California (USC).

These environments utilize an integrated combination of intelligent tutoring system and serious game technologies. Trainees work through a series of interactive lessons and exercises, called the Skill Builder, focusing on mission-oriented communication skills. The lessons make extensive use of automated speech recognition focused on learner language, and provide learners with feedback on their performance. Cultural notes describing customs and nonverbal gestures are integrated into the Skill Builder lessons. Trainees apply their skills in an interactive Arcade Game, where they use spoken commands in the target language to navigate a town grid, and in a Mission Game, where they participate in real-time dialog with simulated local people in order to accomplish their mission.

2 Systems that Impact Learners

Five TLCTS/OLCTS training courses have been developed so far: Tactical Iraqi™, focusing on Iraqi Arabic, Tactical Pashto™ and Tactical Dari™ focusing on the predominant dialects spoken in Afghanistan, Tactical French™ for Sahel Africa, and Operational Indonesian™. TLCTS courses are complete training courses, providing all of the training materials needed to conduct basic training in foreign language and culture. For example, Tactical Iraqi™ includes eighteen Mission Game scenes, ten Arcade Game levels, and sixty-three Skill Builder scenes comprising over 2000 lesson pages. Additional scenes and lessons are under development.

While the platform imposes no limit on content size, the material developed so far or these systems typically covers 80-120 hours of training. In-game reference materials, including glossaries, summaries of lesson content, and grammar notes, are

Proceedings of the NAACL HLT 2010: Demonstration Session, pages 29–32,
Los Angeles, California, June 2010.

available both as part of the training package and as is a support Web site. Manuals, comprising tutorials and training guidelines, help with initial orientation, training management, and troubleshooting. The OLCTS versions of these courses include supplementary exercises delivered on handheld devices and on the web, giving trainees a range of platforms for "train-anywhere" access.

TLCTS rapidly transitioned into widespread use. Computer labs for training with TLCTS courses have been established in numerous locations in the USA and around the world. An estimated twenty-five thousand US military users have trained with the system, and consistently rate it highly. It has also been made available to service members in allied military forces.

Although the Tactical Language and Culture concept was originally developed under military funding, the approach can be applied quite generally to language and culture learning. The key is that the courses are task-oriented: the learner has a task to carry out, the Skill Builder helps the learner to acquire the skills necessary to carry out the task, and the Mission Game gives the learner an opportunity to practice the task in compelling simulated settings.

3 Conversational Agent Technologies

Simulated dialogs are executed by the virtual human architecture described in (Johnson & Valente, 2008). The architecture adopts a variant of the SAIBA framework (Vilhjalmsson & Marsella, 2005), which separates intent planning (the choice of what to communicate) from production of believable behavior (how to realize the communication). An overview of the social simulation process is given in Figure 1.

3.1 Rule-Driven Behavior

Virtual human behavior is generated by a series of components that include explicit models of speech and language (for natural language understanding and generation) as well as behavior-mapping rules that implicitly reflect the subject-matter expertise of the rule authors. These rules generally occur at the level of communicative acts (Traum & Hinkelman, 1992). A simple example of such a rule, expressed in natural language, is shown below:

IF the learner says that your home is beautiful,
THEN reply that it is quite plain (1)

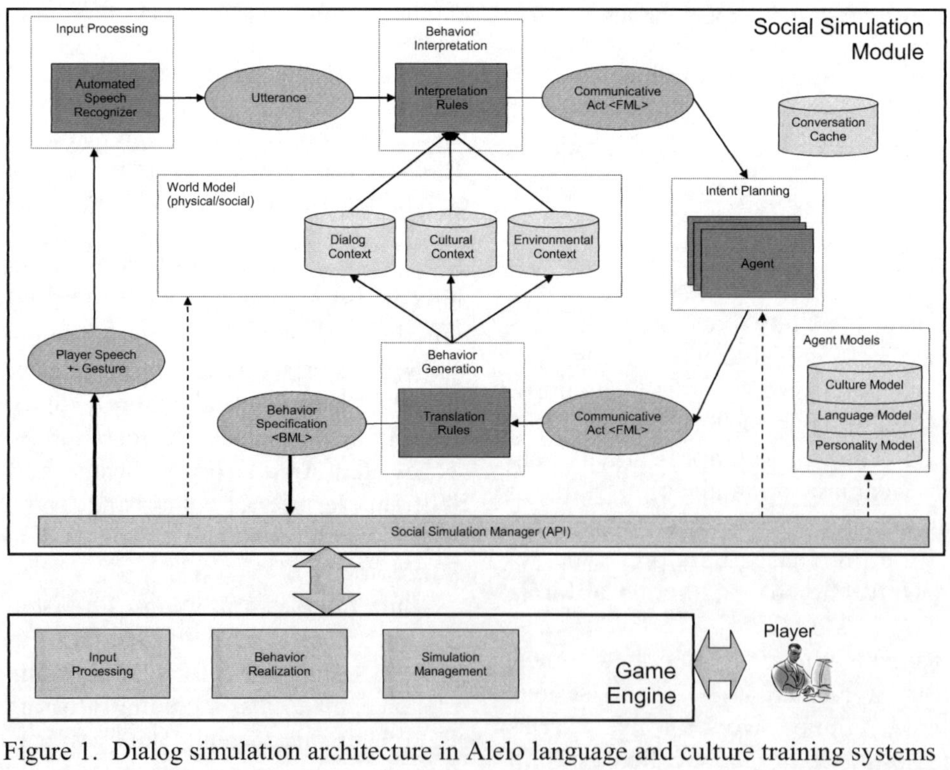

Figure 1. Dialog simulation architecture in Alelo language and culture training systems

Figure 2. Screen shot of a Mission Game dialog in Operational Dari™

3.2 Collaborative Authoring

Rules like (1) are created by a content development team with expertise in linguistics and cultural anthropology. This work is supported by a set of web-based collaborative authoring tools, called Kona and TIDE. Kona is used to create lesson content for the Skill Builder, while TIDE is a graphical editor used to encode dialog rules as transitions in a Finite State Machine.

Kona gives authors access to a database of lesson content, specified in XML format. The authors can selectively lock and edit lessons in the database, and view and edit different fields in the specification of each page in the lesson. The author can edit the written descriptions of the image on the page, the cultural notes, and the enabling learning objectives (ELOs) covered in the page. In other views, authors can link in images and sound recordings, and make notes and comments for other authors to review. The lesson specifications are then automatically translated into the internal data format used in OLCTS, so that authors can review the lessons as they appear in the training application.

4 The Demonstration

The demonstration will give participants an opportunity to use OLCTS, and other Alelo interactive language and culture training products, and learn about their supporting authoring tools. It is intended for people who are interested in gaining an in-depth understanding of AIED (artificial intelligence in education) technology for serious games, and the development tools used to create them. The demo will be conducted by a presenter, who will give live demonstrations of the software, and an assistant presenter who will coach the participants in the use of the game and supporting authoring tools.

4.1 Overview

First, the participants will get a hands-on introduction to one of the Operational Language and Culture courses. Under supervision of a presenter, the participants will learn to say a few phrases in the Skill Builder and use the phrases that they have learned in the Mission Game. This portion can be tailored on the fly to the interests of participants, and can take from 5 to 30 minutes to complete.

Depending on time and interest, participants may also have an opportunity to work with an OLCTS course in more depth. They can be called upon to learn some basic communication skills in Dari and apply them in the Mission Game. This will give participants a firsthand understanding of how each component of OLCTS supports learning, how the components support each other, and how artificial intelligence technology is applied in the learning experience.

Finally, the presenter will demo some of the authoring tools used to create OLCTS content. The participants will propose modifications or extensions to an existing OLCTS course. The presenter will use the authoring tools in real time to make the modifications, following the recommendations of the participants.

4.2 Example: Engaging in a Dialog in Operational Dari™

For a video summary of the demonstration, please visit http://www.alelo.com/movie_tlt-6min.html. The user experience in the Mission Game is one engaging component of this demonstration. An example script for a Mission Game interaction in Alelo's Operational Dari™ course is given in the following sections.

A sample of a Mission Game screen is shown in Figure 2. The player controls the figure in the center-left. At this point in the demonstration, the player has received a briefing that describes a communication task that he or she should accomplish in this exercise. To complete the task, the player must engage the virtual human, or non-player character (NPC) shown on the right.

Organizing rebuilding operations is one example of such a task. The NPC is a host-national character in Afghanistan. The player should check on the status of their shared plan for rebuilding and give constructive feedback. This type of communication task can require finesse and delicacy on the part of the player in order to be culturally appropriate. It draws on the learner's understanding and skill with face-saving, a prominent feature of many cultures worldwide.

The learner must initiate the conversation by speaking into a headset-mounted microphone. He or she clicks on the microphone icon, shown in Figure 3, speaks, then clicks on the icon again to indicate the end of the turn.

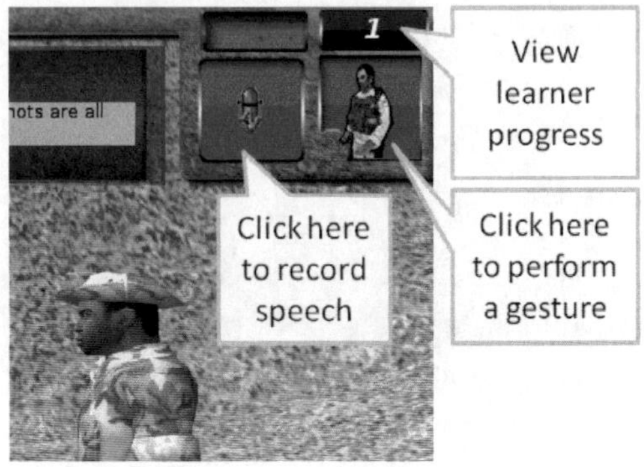

Figure 2. Push the microphone button to speak during a dialog, push again to stop.

Recognized player speech is posted to a dialog history window that appears near the top of the virtual scene, as shown in Figure 1. The NPC responds using spoken output, creating a realistic and engaging practice environment. During the dialog, the player may view hints that display key phrases in Dari. Once the player has discussed all of the host national's training mistakes, the dialog ends in success.

References

H. Vilhjalmsson and S. Marsella. "Social Performance Framework", in *Proceedings of the AAAI Workshop on Modular Construction of Human-Like Intelligence*. 2005.

W. L. Johnson and A. Valente. "Tactical Language and Culture Training Systems: Using Artificial Intelligence to Teach Foreign Languages and Cultures", in *Proceedings of IAAI 2008*. March 2008.

David R. Traum and Elizabeth A. Hinkelman. "Conversation Acts in Task-Oriented Spoken Dialogue", in *Computational Intelligence*, 8(3):575--599, 1992.

Interpretation of Partial Utterances in Virtual Human Dialogue Systems

Kenji Sagae and **David DeVault** and **David R. Traum**
Institute for Creative Technologies
University of Southern California
Marina del Rey, CA 90292, USA
{sagae,devault,traum}@ict.usc.edu

Abstract

Dialogue systems typically follow a rigid pace of interaction where the system waits until the user has finished speaking before producing a response. Interpreting user utterances before they are completed allows a system to display more sophisticated conversational behavior, such as rapid turn-taking and appropriate use of backchannels and interruptions. We demonstrate a natural language understanding approach for partial utterances, and its use in a virtual human dialogue system that can often complete a user's utterances in real time.

1 Introduction

In a typical spoken dialogue system pipeline, the results of automatic speech recognition (ASR) for each user utterance are sent to modules that perform natural language understanding (NLU) and dialogue management only after the utterance is complete. This results in a rigid and often unnatural pacing where the system must wait until the user stops speaking before trying to understand and react to user input. To achieve more flexible turn-taking with human users, for whom turn-taking and feedback at the sub-utterance level is natural, the system needs the ability to start interpretation of user utterances before they are completed.

We demonstrate an implementation of techniques we have developed for partial utterance understanding in virtual human dialogue systems (Sagae et al., 2009; DeVault et al., 2009) with the goal of equipping these systems with sophisticated conversational behavior, such as interruptions and non-verbal feedback. Our demonstration highlights the understanding of utterances before they are finished. It also includes an utterance completion capability, where a virtual human can make a strategic decision to display its understanding of an unfinished user utterance by completing the utterance itself.

The work we demonstrate here is part of a growing research area in which new technical approaches to incremental utterance processing are being developed (e.g. Schuler et al. (2009), Kruijff et al. (2007)), new possible metrics for evaluating the performance of incremental processing are being proposed (e.g. Schlangen et al. (2009)), and the advantages for dialogue system performance and usability are starting to be empirically quantified (e.g. Skantze and Schlangen (2009), Aist et al. (2007)).

2 NLU for partial utterances

In previous work (Sagae et al., 2009), we presented an approach for prediction of semantic content from partial speech recognition hypotheses, looking at length of the speech hypothesis as a general indicator of semantic accuracy in understanding. In subsequent work (DeVault et al., 2009), we incorporated additional features of real-time incremental interpretation to develop a more nuanced prediction model that can accurately identify moments of maximal understanding within individual spoken utterances. This research was conducted in the context of the SASO-EN virtual human dialogue system (Traum et al., 2008), using a corpus of approximately 4,500 utterances from user sessions. The corpus includes a recording of each original utterance, a

Proceedings of the NAACL HLT 2010: Demonstration Session, pages 33–36,

$$\begin{bmatrix} mood: declarative & \\ sem: & \begin{bmatrix} type: event \\ agent: captain-kirk \\ event: deliver \\ theme: power-generator \\ modal: \begin{bmatrix} possibility: can \end{bmatrix} \\ speech-act: \begin{bmatrix} type: offer \end{bmatrix} \end{bmatrix} \end{bmatrix}$$

Figure 1: AVM utterance representation.

manual transcription, and a gold-standard semantic frame, allowing us to develop and evaluate a data-driven NLU approach.

2.1 NLU in SASO-EN Virtual Humans

Our NLU module for the SASO-EN system, mxNLU (Sagae et al., 2009), is based on maximum entropy classification (Berger et al., 1996) , where we treat entire individual semantic frames as classes, and extract input features from ASR. The NLU output representation is an attribute-value matrix (AVM), where the attributes and values represent semantic information that is linked to a domain-specific ontology and task model (Figure 1). The AVMs are linearized, using a path-value notation, as seen in the NLU input-output example below:

- Utterance (speech): *we are prepared to give you guys generators for electricity downtown*
- ASR (NLU input): *we up apparently give you guys generators for a letter city don town*
- Frame (NLU output):

```
<s>.mood declarative
<s>.sem.type event
<s>.sem.agent captain-kirk
<s>.sem.event deliver
<s>.sem.theme power-generator
<s>.sem.modal.possibility can
<s>.sem.speechact.type offer
```

When mxNLU is trained on complete ASR output for approximately 3,500 utterances, and tested on a separate set of 350 complete ASR utterances, the F-score of attribute-value pairs produced by the NLU is 0.76 (0.78 precision and 0.74 recall). These figures reflect the use of ASR at run-time, and most errors are caused by incorrect speech recognition.

2.2 NLU with partial ASR results (Sagae et al., 2009)

To interpret utterances before they are complete, we use partial recognition hypotheses produced by ASR every 200 milliseconds while the user is speaking. To process these partial utterances produced by ASR, we train length-specific models for mxNLU. These models are trained using the partial ASR results we obtain by running ASR on the audio corresponding to the utterances in the training data. The NLU task is then to predict the meaning of the entire utterance based only on a (noisy) prefix of the utterance. On average, the accuracy of mxNLU on a six-word prefix of an utterance (0.74 F-score) is almost as the same as the accuracy of mxNLU on entire utterances. Approximately half of the utterances in our corpus contain more than six words, creating interesting opportunities for conversational behavior that would be impossible under a model where each utterance must be completed before it is interpreted.

2.3 Detecting points of maximal understanding (DeVault et al., 2009)

Although length-specific NLU models produce accurate results on average, more effective use of the interpretation provided by these models might be achieved if we could automatically gauge their performance on individual utterances at run-time. To that end, we have developed an approach (DeVault et al., 2009) that aims to detect those strategic points in time, as specific utterances are occurring, when the system reaches maximal understanding of the utterance, in the sense that its interpretation will not significantly improve during the rest of the utterance.

Figure 2 illustrates the incremental output of mxNLU as a user asks, *elder do you agree to move the clinic downtown?* Our ASR processes captured audio in 200ms chunks. The figure shows the partial ASR results after the ASR has processed each 200ms of audio, along with the F-score achieved by mxNLU on each of these partials. Note that the NLU F-score fluctuates somewhat as the ASR revises its incremental hypotheses about the user utterance, but generally increases over time.

For the purpose of initiating an overlapping response to a user utterance such as this one, the agent needs to be able (in the right circumstances) to make

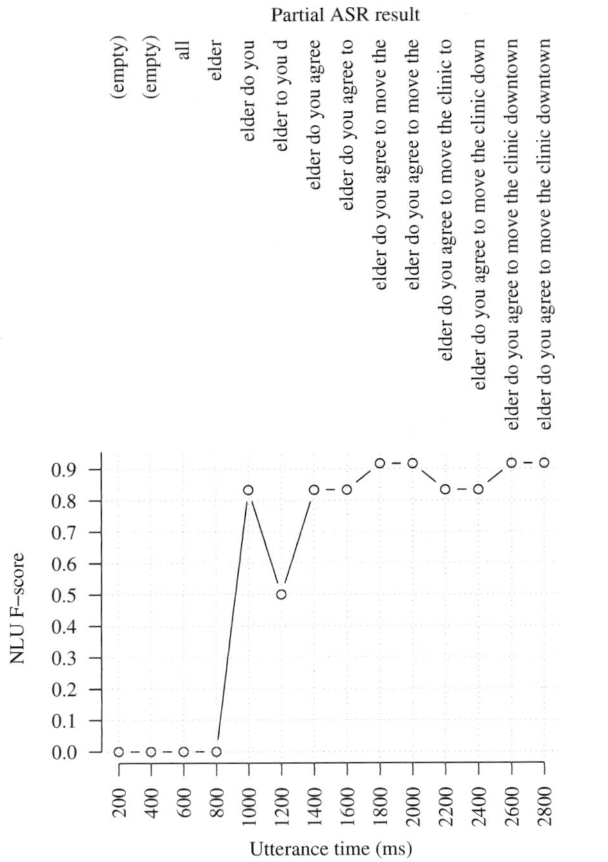

Figure 2: Incremental interpretation of a user utterance.

an assessment that it has already understood the utterance "well enough", based on the partial ASR results that are currently available. We have implemented a specific approach to this assessment which views an utterance as understood "well enough" if the agent would not understand the utterance any better than it currently does even if it were to wait for the user to finish their utterance (and for the ASR to finish interpreting the complete utterance).

Concretely, Figure 2 shows that after the entire 2800ms utterance has been processed by the ASR, mxNLU achieves an F-score of 0.91. However, in fact, mxNLU already achieves this maximal F-score at the moment it interprets the partial ASR result *elder do you agree to move the* at 1800ms. The agent therefore could, in principle, initiate an overlapping response at 1800ms without sacrificing any accuracy in its understanding of the user's utterance.

Of course the agent does not automatically realize that it has achieved a maximal F-score at 1800ms. To enable the agent to make this assessment, we have trained a classifier, which we call MAXF, that can be invoked for any specific partial ASR result, and which uses various features of the ASR result and the current mxNLU output to estimate whether the NLU F-score for the current partial ASR result is at least as high as the mxNLU F-score would be if the agent were to wait for the entire utterance.

To facilitate training of a MAXF classifier, we identified a range of potentially useful features that the agent could use at run-time to assess its confidence in mxNLU's output for a given partial ASR result. These features include: the number of partial results that have been received from the ASR; the length (in words) of the current partial ASR result; the entropy in the probability distribution mxNLU assigns to alternative output frames (lower entropy corresponds to a more focused distribution); the probability mxNLU assigns to the most probable output frame; and the most probable output frame.

Based on these features, we trained a decision tree to make the binary prediction that MAXF is TRUE or FALSE for each partial ASR result. DeVault et al. (2009) include a detailed evaluation and discussion of the classifier. To briefly summarize our results, the precision/recall/F-score of the trained MAXF model are 0.88/0.52/0.65 respectively. The high precision means that 88% of the time that the model predicts that F-score is maximized at a specific partial, it really is. Our demonstration, which we outline in the next section, highlights the utility of a high-precision MAXF classifier in making the decision whether to complete a user's utterance.

3 Demo script outline

We have implemented the approach for partial utterance understanding described above in the SASO-EN system (Traum et al., 2008), a virtual human dialogue system with speech input and output (Figure 3), allowing us to demonstrate both partial utterance understanding and some of the specific behaviors made possible by this capability. We divide this demonstration in two parts: visualization of NLU for partial utterances and user utterance completion.

Figure 3: SASO-EN: Dr. Perez and Elder al-Hassan.

Partial ASR result	*Predicted completion*
we can provide transportation	to move the patient there
the market is not	safe
there are supplies	where we are going

Table 1: Examples of user utterance completions.

3.1 Visualization of NLU for partial utterances

Because the demonstration depends on usage of the system within the domain for which it was designed, the demo operator provides a brief description of the system, task and domain. The demo operator (or a volunteer user) then speaks normally to the system, while a separate window visualizes the system's evolving understanding. This display is updated every 200 milliseconds, allowing attendees to see partial utterance understanding in action. For ease of comprehension, the display will summarize the NLU state using an English paraphrase of the predicted meaning (rather than displaying the structured frame that is the actual output of NLU). The display will also visualize the TRUE or FALSE state of the MAXF classifier, highlighting the moment the system thinks it reaches maximal understanding.

3.2 User utterance completion

The demo operator (or volunteer user) starts to speak and pauses briefly in mid-utterance, at which point, if possible, one of the virtual humans jumps in and completes the utterance (DeVault et al., 2009). Table 1 includes a few examples of the many utterances that can be completed by the virtual humans.

4 Conclusion

Interpretation of partial utterances, combined with a way to predict points of maximal understanding, opens exciting possibilities for more natural conversational behavior in virtual humans. This demonstration showcases the NLU approach and a sample application of the basic techniques.

Acknowledgments

The work described here has been sponsored by the U.S. Army Research, Development, and Engineering Command (RDECOM). Statements and opinions expressed do not necessarily reflect the position or the policy of the United States Government, and no official endorsement should be inferred.

References

G. Aist, J. Allen, E. Campana, C. G. Gallo, S. Stoness, M. Swift, and M. K. Tanenhaus. 2007. Incremental dialogue system faster than and preferred to its non-incremental counterpart. In *Proc. of the 29th Annual Conference of the Cognitive Science Society*.

A. Berger, S. Della Pietra, and V. Della Pietra. 1996. A maximum entropy approach to natural language processing. *Computational Linguistics*, 22(1):39–71.

D. DeVault, K. Sagae, and D. Traum. 2009. Can I finish? Learning when to respond to incremental interpretation results in interactive dialogue. In *Proc. SIGDIAL*.

G. J. Kruijff, P. Lison, T. Benjamin, H. Jacobsson, and N. Hawes. 2007. Incremental, multi-level processing for comprehending situated dialogue in human-robot interaction. In *Proc. LangRo'2007*.

K. Sagae, G. Christian, D. DeVault, and D. R. Traum. 2009. Towards natural language understanding of partial speech recognition results in dialogue systems. In Short Paper Proceedings of NAACL HLT.

D. Schlangen, T. Baumann, and M. Atterer. 2009. Incremental reference resolution: The task, metrics for evaluation, and a Bayesian filtering model that is sensitive to disfluencies. In *Proc. SIGDIAL*, page 30–37.

W. Schuler, S. Wu, and L. Schwartz. 2009. A framework for fast incremental interpretation during speech decoding. *Computational Linguistics*, 35(3):313–343.

G. Skantze and D. Schlangen. 2009. Incremental dialogue processing in a micro-domain. In *Proc. EACL*.

D. Traum, S. Marsella, J. Gratch, J. Lee, and A. Hartholt. 2008. Multi-party, multi-issue, multi-strategy negotiation for multi-modal virtual agents. In *Proc. of the Eighth International Conference on Intelligent Virtual Agents*.

Interactive Predictive Parsing using a Web-based Architecture*

Ricardo Sánchez-Sáez† **Luis A. Leiva**‡ **Joan-Andreu Sánchez**† **José-Miguel Benedí**†

Instituto Tecnológico de Informática
Universidad Politécnica de Valencia

{rsanchez,luileito,jandreu,jbenedi}@{†dsic,‡iti}.upv.es

Abstract

This paper introduces a Web-based demonstration of an interactive-predictive framework for syntactic tree annotation, where the user is tightly integrated into the interactive parsing system. In contrast with the traditional post-editing approach, both the user and the system cooperate to generate error-free annotated trees. User feedback is provided by means of natural mouse gestures and keyboard strokes.

1 Introduction

There is a whole family of problems within the parsing world where error-free results, in the form of perfectly annotated trees, are needed. Constructing error-free trees is a necessity in many tasks, such as handwritten mathematical expression recognition (Yamamoto et al., 2006), or new gold standard treebank creation (de la Clergerie et al., 2008). It is a fact that current state-of-the-art syntactic parsers provide trees that, although of excellent quality, still contain errors. Because of this, the figure of a human corrector who supervises the annotation process is unavoidable in this kind of problems.

When using automatic parsers as a baseline for building perfect syntactic trees, the role of the human annotator is to post-edit the trees and correct the errors. This manner of operating results in the typical two-step process for error correcting, in which the system first generates the whole output and then the user verifies or amends it. This paradigm is rather inefficient and uncomfortable for the human annotator. For example, in the creation of the Penn Treebank annotated corpus, a basic two-stage setup was employed: a rudimentary parsing system provided a skeletal syntactic representation, which then was manually corrected by human annotators (Marcus et al., 1994). Other tree annotating tools within the two-step paradigm exist, such as the TreeBanker (Carter, 1997) or the Tree Editor TrEd[1].

With the objective of reducing the user effort and making this laborious task easier, we devised an Interactive Predictive framework. Our aim is to put the user into the loop, embedding him as a part of the automatic parser, and allowing him to interact in real time within the system. In this manner, the system can use the readily available user feedback to make predictions about the parts that have not been validated by the corrector.

In this paper, we present a Web-based demo, which implements the Interactive Predictive Parsing (IPP) framework presented in (Sánchez-Sáez et al., 2009). User feedback (provided by means of keyboard and mouse operations) allows the system to predict new subtrees for unvalidated parts of the annotated sentence, which in turn reduces the human effort and improves annotation efficiency.

As a back-end for our demo, we use a more polished version of the CAT-API library, the Web-based Computer Assisted Tool introduced in (Alabau et al., 2009). This library allows for a clean application design, in which both the server side (the parsing engine) and the client side (which draws the trees, captures and interprets the user feedback, and requests

*Work partially supported by the Spanish MICINN under the MIPRCV "Consolider Ingenio 2010" (CSD2007-00018), MITTRAL (TIN2009-14633-C03-01), Prometeo (PROMETEO/2009/014) research projects, and the FPU fellowship AP2006-01363. The authors wish to thank Vicent Alabau for his invaluable help with the CAT-API library.

[1] *http://ufal.mff.cuni.cz/~pajas/tred/*

Proceedings of the NAACL HLT 2010: Demonstration Session, pages 37–40,
Los Angeles, California, June 2010.

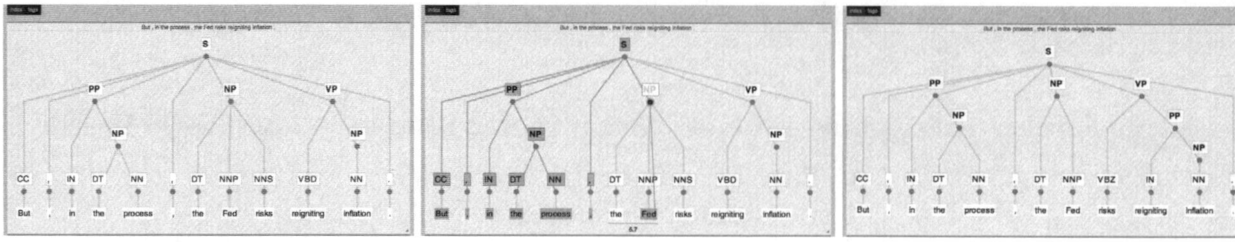

(a) System: output tree 1 (b) User: *span modification* (c) System: output tree 2

Figure 1: An interaction example on the IPP system.

parsed subtrees to the server) are independent. One of the features that steam from the CAT-API library is the ability for several annotators to work concurrently on the same problem-set, each in a different client computer sharing the same parsing server.

Interactive predictive methods have been successfully demonstrated to ease the work of transcriptors and translators in fields like Handwriting Text Recognition (Romero et al., 2009; Toselli et al., 2008) and Statistical Machine Translation (Ortiz et al., 2010; Vidal et al., 2006). This new paradigm enables the collaboration between annotators across the globe, granting them a physical and geographical freedom that was inconceivable in the past.

2 Interactive Predictive Parsing

A tree t, associated to a string $x_{1|x|}$, is composed by substructures that are usually referred as constituents. A constituent c_{ij}^{A} is defined by the nonterminal symbol A (either a *syntactic label* or a *POS tag*) and its span ij (the starting and ending indexes which delimit the part of the input sentence encompassed by the constituent).

Here follows a general formulation for the non-interactive parsing scenario. Using a grammatical model G, the parser analyzes the input sentence $\boldsymbol{x} = \{x_1, \ldots, x_{|x|}\}$ and produces the parse tree $\hat{t}$

$$\hat{t} = \arg\max_{t \in \mathcal{T}} p_G(t|\boldsymbol{x}), \tag{1}$$

where $p_G(t|\boldsymbol{x})$ is the probability of parse tree t given the input string $\boldsymbol{x}$ using model G, and $\mathcal{T}$ is the set of all possible parse trees for $\boldsymbol{x}$.

In the interactive predictive scenario, after obtaining the (probably incorrect) best tree $\hat{t}$, the user is able to individually correct any of its constituents c_{ij}^{A}. The system reacts to each of the corrections introduced by the human, proposing a new $\hat{t}'$ that takes into account the afore-mentioned corrections.

The action of modifying an incorrect constituent (either setting the correct span or the correct label) implicitly validates a subtree that is composed by the partially corrected constituent, all of its ancestor constituents, and all constituents whose end span is lower than the start span of the corrected constituent. We will name this subtree the validated prefix tree t_p. When the user replaces the constituent c_{ij}^{A} with the correct one $c_{ij}'^{A}$, the validated prefix tree is:

$$\begin{aligned} t_p(c_{ij}'^{A}) = \{c_{mn}^{B} \ : \ m \leq i, \ n \geq j, \\ d(c_{mn}^{B}) \leq d(c_{ij}'^{A})\} \cup \\ \{c_{pq}^{D} \ : \ p >= 1 \ , \ q < i\} \end{aligned} \tag{2}$$

with $d(c_{mn}^{B})$ being the depth of constituent c_{mn}^{B}.

When a constituent correction is performed, the prefix tree $t_p(c_{ij}'^{A})$ is fixed and a new tree $\hat{t}'$ that takes into account the prefix is proposed

$$\hat{t}' = \arg\max_{t \in \mathcal{T}} p_G(t|\boldsymbol{x}, t_p(c_{ij}'^{A})). \tag{3}$$

Given that we are working with context-free grammars, the only subtree that effectively needs to be recalculated is the one starting from the parent of the corrected constituent.

3 Demo outline

A preview version of the demonstration can be accessed at *http://cat.iti.upv.es/ipp/*.

The user is presented with the sentences in the selected corpus, and starts parsing them one by one. They make corrections in the trees both with the keyboard and the computer mouse. The user feedback is decoded on the client side which in turn requests subtrees to the parse engine.

Two kind of operations can be performed over constituents: span modification (performed either by dragging a line from the constituent to the word that corresponds to the span's upper index, or deleting a tree branch by clicking on it), and label substitution (done by typing the correct one on its text field). Modifying the span of a constituent invalidates its label, so the server recalculates it as part of the suffix. Modifying the label of a constituent validates its span.

When the user is about to perform an operation, the affected constituent and the prefix that will be validated are highlighted. The target span of the modified constituent is visually shown as well. When the user obtains the correctly annotated tree, they can accept it by by clicking on a new sentence.

As already mentioned, the user is tightly integrated into the interactive parsing process. They follow a predetermined protocol in which they correct and/or validate the annotated parse trees:

1. The parsing server proposes a full parse tree t for the input sentence. The tree t is shown to the user by the client (Fig. 1a).

2. The user finds the first[2] incorrect constituent c and starts amending it, either by changing its label or changing its span (Fig. 1b, note how the label is greyed out as it is discarded with the span modification). This operation implicitly validates the prefix tree t_p (highlighted in green).

3. The system decodes the user feedback (i.e., mouse gestures or keyboard strokes) which can either affect the label or the span of the incorrect constituent c:

   (a) If the span of c is modified, the label is not assumed to be correct. A partial constituent c^*, which includes *span* but no *label*, is decoded from the user feedback.

   (b) If the label of c is modified, the span is assumed to be correct. The corrected constituent c' is decoded from the user feedback.

   This step only deals with analysing the user feedback, the parsing server will not be contacted until the next step.

4. Either the partially corrected constituent c^* or the corrected constituent c' is then used by the client to create a new *extended consolidated prefix* that combines the validated prefix and the user feedback: either t_pc^* or t_pc'. The client sends the extended prefix tree to the parsing server and requests a suitable continuation for the parse tree, or tree suffix t_s:

   (a) If the extended prefix is partial (t_pc^*), the first element of t_s is the label completing c^*, followed by the remaining calculated whole constituents.

   (b) If the extended prefix is complete (t_pc'), the parsing server produces a suitable tree suffix t_s which contains the remaining calculated whole constituents.

5. The client concatenates the suffix returned by the server to the validated extended prefix, and shows the whole tree to the client (Fig. 1c).

6. These previous steps are iterated until a final, perfect parse tree is produced by the server and validated by the user.

Note that within this protocol, constituents can be deleted or inserted by adequately modifying the span of the left-neighbouring constituent.

4 Demo architecture

The proposed system coordinates client-side scripting with server-side technologies, by using the CAT-API library (Alabau et al., 2009).

4.1 Server side

The server side of our system is a parsing engine based on a customized CYK-Viterbi parser, which uses a Probabilistic Context-Free Grammar in Chomsky Normal Form obtained from sections 2 to 21 of the UPenn Treebank as a model (see (Sánchez-Sáez et al., 2009) for details).

The client can request to the parsing server the best subtree for any given span of the input string. For each requested subtree, the client can either provide the starting label or not. If the starting subtree

[2]The tree visiting order is left-to-right depth-first.

label is not provided, the server calculates the most probable label. The server also performs transparent tree debinarization/binarization when communicating with the client.

4.2 Client side

The client side has been designed taking into account ergonomic issues in order to facilitate the interaction.

The prototype is accessed through a Web browser, and the only requirement is the Flash plugin (98% of market penetration) installed in the client machine. The hardware requirements in the client are very low on the client side, as the parsing is process performed remotely on the server side: any computer (including netbooks) capable of running a modern Web browser is enough.

Each validated user interaction is saved as a log file on the server side, so a tree's annotation session can be later resumed.

4.2.1 Communication protocol

This demo exploits the WWW to enable the connection of simultaneous accesses across the globe. This architecture also provides cross-platform compatibility and requires neither computational power nor disk space on the client's machine.

Client and server communicate via asynchronous HTTP connections, providing thus a richer interactive experience – no page refreshes is required when parsing a new sentence. Moreover, the Web client communicates with the IPP engine through binary TCP sockets. Thus, response times are quite slow – a desired requirement for the user's solace. Additionally, cross-domain requests are possible, so the user could switch between different IPP engines within the same UI.

5 Evaluation results

We have carried out experiments that simulate user interaction using section 23 of the Penn Treebank. The results suggest figures ranging from 42% to 46% of effort saving compared to manually post-editing the trees without an interactive system. In other words, for every 100 erroneous constituents produced by a parsing system, an IPP user would correct only 58 (the other 42 constituents being automatically recalculated by the IPP system). Again, see (Sánchez-Sáez et al., 2009) for the details on experimentation.

5.1 Conclusions and future work

We have introduced a Web-based interactive-predictive system that, by using a parse engine in an integrated manner, aids the user in creating correctly annotated syntactic trees. Our system greatly reduces the human effort required for this task compared to using a non-interactive automatic system.

Future work includes improvements to the client side (e.g., confidence measures as a visual aid, multimodality), as well as exploring other kinds of parsing algorithms for the server side (e.g., adaptative parsing).

References

V. Alabau, D. Ortiz, V. Romero, and J. Ocampo. 2009. A multimodal predictive-interactive application for computer assisted transcription and translation. In *ICMI-MLMI '09*, 227–228.

D. Carter. 1997. The TreeBanker. A tool for supervised training of parsed corpora. In *ENVGRAM'97*, 9–15.

E.V. de la Clergerie, O. Hamon, D. Mostefa, C. Ayache, P. Paroubek, and A. Vilnat. 2008. Passage: from French parser evaluation to large sized treebank. In *LREC'08*, 100:P2.

M.P. Marcus, B. Santorini, and M.A. Marcinkiewicz. 1994. Building a large annotated corpus of English: The Penn Treebank. *Computational linguistics*, 19(2):313–330.

D. Ortiz, L. A. Leiva, V. Alabau, and F. Casacuberta. 2010. Interactive machine translation using a web-based architecture. In *IUI'10*, 423–425.

V. Romero, L. A. Leiva, A. H. Toselli, and E. Vidal. 2009. Interactive multimodal transcription of text imagse using a web-based demo system. In *IUI'09*, 477–478.

R. Sánchez-Sáez, J.A. Sánchez, and J.M. Benedí. 2009. Interactive predictive parsing. In *IWPT'09*, 222–225.

A.H. Toselli, V. Romero, and E. Vidal. 2008. Computer assisted transcription of text images and multimodal interaction. In *MLMI'08*, 5237: 296–308.

E. Vidal, F. Casacuberta, L. Rodríguez, J. Civera, and C. Martínez. 2006. Computer-assisted translation using speech recognition. *IEEE Trans. on Audio, Speech and Language Processing*, 14(3):941–951.

R. Yamamoto, S. Sako, T. Nishimoto, and S. Sagayama. 2006. On-line recognition of handwritten mathematical expressions based on stroke-based stochastic context-free grammar. In *10th Frontiers in Handwriting Recognition*, 249–254.

SIMPLIFICA: a tool for authoring simplified texts in Brazilian Portuguese guided by readability assessments

Carolina Scarton, Matheus de Oliveira, Arnaldo Candido Jr., Caroline Gasperin and Sandra Maria Aluísio
Department of Computer Sciences, University of São Paulo
Av. Trabalhador São-Carlense, 400. 13560-970 - São Carlos/SP, Brazil
{carolina@grad,matheusol@grad,arnaldoc@,cgasperin@,sandra@}icmc.usp.br

Abstract

SIMPLIFICA is an authoring tool for producing simplified texts in Portuguese. It provides functionalities for lexical and syntactic simplification and for readability assessment. This tool is the first of its kind for Portuguese; it brings innovative aspects for simplification tools in general, since the authoring process is guided by readability assessment based on the levels of literacy of the Brazilian population.

1 Introduction

In order to promote digital inclusion and accessibility for people with low levels of literacy, particularly access to documents available on the web, it is important to provide textual information in a simple and easy way. Indeed, the Web Content Accessibility Guidelines (WCAG) 2.0[1] establishes a set of guidelines that discuss accessibility issues and provide accessibility design solutions. WCAG requirements address not only structure and technological aspects, but also how the content should be made available to users. However, Web developers are not always responsible for content preparation and authoring in a Website. Moreover, in the context of Web 2.0 it becomes extremely difficult to develop completely WCAG conformant Websites, since users without any prior knowledge about the guidelines directly participate on the content authoring process of Web applications.

In Brazil, since 2001, the INAF index (National Indicator of Functional Literacy) has been computed annually to measure the levels of literacy of the Brazilian population. The 2009 report presented a still worrying scenario: 7% of the individuals were classified as illiterate; 21% as literate at the rudimentary level; 47% as literate at the basic level; and only 25% as literate at the advanced level (INAF, 2009). These literacy levels are defined as: (1) **Illiterate**: individuals who cannot perform simple tasks such as reading words and phrases; (2) **Rudimentary**: individuals who can find explicit information in short and familiar texts (such as an advertisement or a short letter); (3) **Basic**: individuals who can read and understand texts of average length, and find information even when it is necessary to make some inference; and (4) **Advanced/Fully**: individuals who can read longer texts, relating their parts, comparing and interpreting information, distinguish fact from opinion, make inferences and synthesize.

We present in this paper the current version of an authoring tool named SIMPLIFICA. It helps authors to create simple texts targeted at poor literate readers. It extends the previous version presented in Candido et al. (2009) with two new modules: lexical simplification and the assessment of the level of complexity of the input texts. The study is part of the PorSimples project[2] (Simplification of Portuguese Text for Digital Inclusion and Accessibility) (Aluisio et al., 2008).

This paper is organized as follows. In Section 2

[1] http://www.w3.org/TR/WCAG20/

[2] http://caravelas.icmc.usp.br/wiki/index.php/Principal

Proceedings of the NAACL HLT 2010: Demonstration Session, pages 41–44,
Los Angeles, California, June 2010.

we describe SIMPLIFICA and the underlying technology for lexical and syntactic simplification, and for readability assessment. In Section 3 we summarize the interaction steps that we propose to show in the demonstration session targeting texts for low-literate readers of Portuguese. Section 4 presents final remarks with emphasis on why demonstrating this system is relevant.

2 SIMPLIFICA authoring tool

SIMLIFICA is a web-based WYSIWYG editor, based on TinyMCE web editor[3]. The user inputs a text in the editor and customizes the simplification settings, where he/she can choose: (i) strong simplification, where all the complex syntactic phenomena (see details in Section 2.2) are treated for each sentence, or customized simplification, where the user chooses one or more syntactic simplification phenomena to be treated for each sentence, and (ii) one or more thesauri to be used in the syntactic and lexical simplification processes. Then the user activates the readability assessment module to predict the complexity level of a text. This module maps the text to one of the three levels of literacy defined by INAF: rudimentary, basic or advanced. According to the resulting readability level the user can trigger the lexical and/or syntactic simplifications modules, revise the automatic simplification and restart the cycle by checking the readability level of the current version of the text.

Figure 1 summarizes how the three modules are integrated and below we describe in more detail the SIMPLIFICA modules.

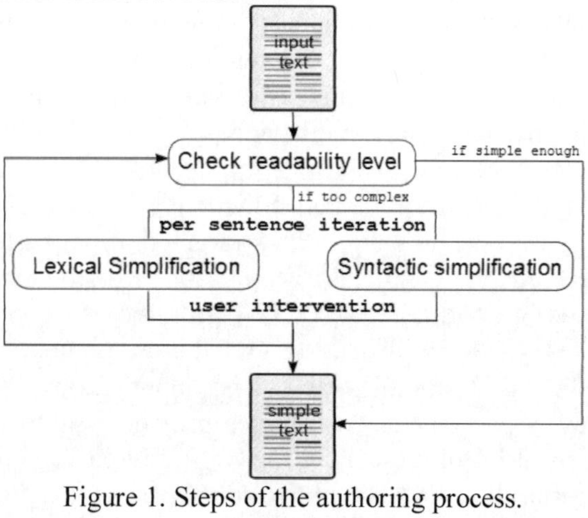

Figure 1. Steps of the authoring process.

[3] http://tinymce.moxiecode.com/

2.1 Lexical Simplification

Basically, the first part of the lexical simplification process consists of tokenizing the original text and marking the words that are considered complex. In order to judge a word as complex or not, we use 3 dictionaries created for the PorSimples project: one containing words common to youngsters, a second one composed by frequent words extracted from news texts for children and nationwide newspapers, and a third one containing concrete words.

The lexical simplification module also uses the Unitex-PB dictionary[4] for finding the lemma of the words in the text, so that it is possible to look for it in the simple words dictionaries. The problem of looking for a lemma directly in a dictionary is that there are ambiguous words and we are not able to deal with different word senses. For dealing with part-of-speech (POS) ambiguity, we use the MXPOST POS tagger[5] trained over NILC tagset[6].

After the text is tagged, the words that are not proper nouns, prepositions and numerals are selected, and their POS tags are used to look for their lemmas in the dictionaries. As the tagger has not a 100% precision and some words may not be in the dictionary, we look for the lemma only (without the tag) when we are not able to find the lemma-tag combination in the dictionary. Still, if we are not able to find the word, the lexical simplification module assumes that the word is complex and marks it for simplification.

The last step of the process consists in providing simpler synonyms for the marked words. For this task, we use the thesauri for Portuguese TeP 2.0[7] and the lexical ontology for Portuguese PAPEL[8]. This task is carried out when the user clicks on a marked word, which triggers a search in the thesauri for synonyms that are also present in the common words dictionary. If simpler words are found, they are listed in order, from the simpler to the more complex ones. To determine this order, we used Google API to search each word in the web: we assume that the higher a word frequency, the simpler it is. Automatic word sense disambiguation is left for future work.

[4] http://www.nilc.icmc.usp.br/nilc/projects/unitex-pb/web/dicionarios.html
[5] http://sites.google.com/site/adwaitratnaparkhi/home
[6] www.nilc.icmc.usp.br/nilc/TagSet/ManualEtiquetagem.htm
[7] http://www.nilc.icmc.usp.br/tep2/
[8] http://www.linguateca.pt/PAPEL/

2.2 Syntactic Simplification

Syntactic simplification is accomplished by a rule-based system, which comprises seven operations that are applied sentence-by-sentence to a text in order to make its syntactic structure simpler.

Our rule-based text simplification system is based on a manual for Brazilian Portuguese syntactic simplification (Specia et al., 2008). According to this manual, simplification operations should be applied when any of the 22 linguistic phenomena covered by our system (see Candido et al. (2009) for details) is detected. Our system treats appositive, relative, coordinate and subordinate clauses, which had already been addressed by previous work on text simplification (Siddharthan, 2003). Additionally, we treat passive voice, sentences in an order other than Subject-Verb-Object (SVO), and long adverbial phrases. The simplification operations available to treat these phenomena are: split sentence, change particular discourse markers by simpler ones, change passive to active voice, invert the order of clauses, convert to subject-verb-object ordering, and move long adverbial phrases.

Each sentence is parsed in order to identify syntactic phenomena for simplification and to segment the sentence into portions that will be handled by the operations. We use the parser PALAVRAS (Bick, 2000) for Portuguese. Gasperin et al. (2010) present the evaluation of the performance of our syntactic simplification system.

Since our syntactic simplifications are conservative, the simplified texts become longer than the original ones due to sentence splitting. We acknowledge that low-literacy readers prefer short texts, and in the future we aim to provide summarization within SIMPLIFICA (see (Watanabe et al., 2009)). Here, the shortening of the text is a responsibility of the author.

2.3 Readability assessment

With our readability assessment module, we can predict the readability level of a text, which corresponds to the literacy level expected from the target reader: rudimentary, basic or advanced.

We have adopted a machine-learning classifier to identify the level of the input text; we use the Support Vector Machines implementation from Weka[9] toolkit (SMO). We have used 7 corpora within 2 different genres (general news and popular science articles) to train the classifier. Three of these corpora contain original texts published in online newspapers and magazines. The other corpora contain manually simplified versions of most of the original texts. These were simplified by a linguist, specialized in text simplification, according to the two levels of simplification proposed in our project, natural and strong, which result in texts adequate for the basic and rudimentary literacy levels, respectively.

Our feature set is composed by cognitively-motivated features derived from the Coh-Metrix-PORT tool[10], which is an adaptation for Brazilian Portuguese of Coh-Metrix 2.0 (free version of Coh-Metrix (Graesser et al, 2003)) also developed in the context of the PorSimples project. Coh-Metrix-PORT implements the metrics in Table 1.

Categories	Subcategories	Metrics
Shallow Readability metric	-	Flesch Reading Ease index for Portuguese.
Words and textual information	Basic counts	Number of words, sentences, paragraphs, words per sentence, sentences per paragraph, syllables per word, incidence of verbs, nouns, adjectives and adverbs.
	Frequencies	Raw frequencies of content words and minimum frequency of content words.
	Hyperonymy	Average number of hypernyms of verbs.
Syntactic information	Constituents	Incidence of nominal phrases, modifiers per noun phrase and words preceding main verbs.
	Pronouns, Types and Tokens	Incidence of personal pronouns, number of pronouns per noun phrase, types and tokens.
	Connectives	Number of connectives, number of positive and negative additive connectives, causal / temporal / logical positive and negative connectives.
Logical operators	-	Incidence of the particles "e" (and), "ou" (or), "se" (if), incidence of negation and logical operators.

Table 1. Metrics of Coh-Metrix-PORT.

[9] http://www.cs.waikato.ac.nz/ml/weka/

[10] http://caravelas.icmc.usp.br:3000/

We also included seven new metrics to Coh-Metrix-PORT: average verb, noun, adjective and adverb ambiguity, incidence of high-level constituents, content words and functional words.

We measured the performance of the classifier on identifying the levels of the input texts by a cross-validation experiment. We trained the classifier on our 7 corpora and reached 90% F-measure on identifying texts at advanced level, 48% at basic level, and 73% at rudimentary level.

3. A working session at SIMPLIFICA

In the NAACL demonstration section we aim to present all functionalities of the tool for authoring simple texts, SIMPLIFICA. We will run all steps of the authoring process – readability assessment, lexical simplification and syntactic simplification – in order to demonstrate the use of the tool in producing a text for basic and rudimentary readers of Portuguese, regarding the lexical and the syntactic complexity of an original text.

We outline a script of our demonstration at http://www.nilc.icmc.usp.br/porsimples/demo/demo_script.htm. In order to help the understanding by non-speakers of Portuguese we provide the translations of the example texts shown.

4. Final Remarks

A tool for authoring simple texts in Portuguese is an innovative software, as are all the modules that form the tool. Such tool is extremely important in the construction of texts understandable by the majority of the Brazilian population. SIMPLIFICA's target audience is varied and includes: teachers that use online text for reading practices; publishers; journalists aiming to reach poor literate readers; content providers for distance learning programs; government agencies that aim to communicate to the population as a whole; companies that produce technical manuals and medicine instructions; users of legal language, in order to facilitate the understanding of legal documents by lay people; and experts in language studies and computational linguistics for future research.

Future versions of SIMPLIFICA will also provide natural simplification, where the target sentences for simplifications are chosen by a machine learning classifier (Gasperin et al., 2009).

Acknowledgments

We thank FAPESP and Microsoft Research for supporting the PorSimples project

References

Sandra Aluísio, Lucia Specia, Thiago Pardo, Erick Maziero and Renata Fortes. 2008. *Towards Brazilian Portuguese Automatic Text Simplification Systems*. In Proceedings of The Eight ACM Symposium on Document Engineering (DocEng 2008), 240-248, São Paulo, Brasil.

Eckhard Bick. 2000. *The Parsing System "Palavras": Automatic Grammatical Analysis of Portuguese in a Constraint Grammar Framework*. PhD thesis. Aarhus University.

Arnaldo Candido Junior, Erick Maziero, Caroline Gasperin, Thiago Pardo, Lucia Specia and Sandra M. Aluisio. 2009. *Supporting the Adaptation of Texts for Poor Literacy Readers: a Text Simplification Editor for Brazilian Portuguese*. In the Proceedings of the NAACL HLT Workshop on Innovative Use of NLP for Building Educational Applications, pages 34–42, Boulder, Colorado, June 2009.

Caroline Gasperin; Lucia Specia; Tiago Pereira and Sandra Aluísio. 2009. *Learning When to Simplify Sentences for Natural Text Simplification*. In: Proceedings of ENIA 2009, 809-818.

Caroline Gasperin, Erick Masiero and Sandra M. Aluisio. 2010. Challenging choices for text simplification. Accepted for publication in Propor 2010 (http://www.inf.pucrs.br/~propor2010/).

Arthur Graesser, Danielle McNamara, Max Louwerse and Zhiqiang Cai. 2004. Coh-Metrix: Analysis of text on cohesion and language. In: *Behavioral Research Methods, Instruments, and Computers*, 36, páginas 193-202.

INAF. 2009. Instituto P. Montenegro and Ação Educativa. *INAF Brasil - Indicador de Alfabetismo Funcional - 2009*. Online available at http://www.ibope.com.br/ipm/relatorios/relatorio_inaf_2009.pdf

Advaith Siddharthan. 2003. *Syntactic Simplification and Text Cohesion*. PhD Thesis. University of Cambridge.

Lucia Specia, Sandra Aluisio and Tiago Pardo. 2008. *Manual de Simplificação Sintática para o Português*. Technical Report NILC-TR-08-06, 27 p. Junho 2008, São Carlos-SP.

Willian Watanabe, Arnaldo Candido Junior, Vinícius Uzêda, Renata Fortes, Tiago Pardo and Sandra Aluísio. 2009. *Facilita: reading assistance for low-literacy readers*. In Proceedings of the 27th ACM International Conference on Design of Communication. SIGDOC '09. ACM, New York, NY, 29-36.

An Overview of Microsoft Web N-gram Corpus and Applications

Kuansan Wang Christopher Thrasher Evelyne Viegas
Xiaolong Li Bo-june (Paul) Hsu
Microsoft Research
One Microsoft Way
Redmond, WA, 98052, USA
webngram@microsoft.com

Abstract

This document describes the properties and some applications of the Microsoft Web N-gram corpus. The corpus is designed to have the following characteristics. First, in contrast to static data distribution of previous corpus releases, this N-gram corpus is made publicly available as an XML Web Service so that it can be updated as deemed necessary by the user community to include new words and phrases constantly being added to the Web. Secondly, the corpus makes available various sections of a Web document, specifically, the body, title, and anchor text, as separates models as text contents in these sections are found to possess significantly different statistical properties and therefore are treated as distinct languages from the language modeling point of view. The usages of the corpus are demonstrated here in two NLP tasks: phrase segmentation and word breaking.

1 Introduction

Since Banko and Brill's pioneering work almost a decade ago (Banko and Brill 2001), it has been widely observed that the effectiveness of statistical natural language processing (NLP) techniques is highly susceptible to the data size used to develop them. As empirical studies have repeatedly shown that simple algorithms can often outperform their more complicated counterparts in wide varieties of NLP applications with large datasets, many have come to believe that it is the size of data, not the sophistication of the algorithms that ultimately play the central role in modern NLP (Norvig, 2008). Towards this end, there have been considerable efforts in the NLP community to gather ever larger datasets, culminating the release of the English Giga-word corpus (Graff and Cieri, 2003) and the 1 Tera-word Google N-gram (Thorsten and Franz, 2006) created from arguably the largest text source available, the World Wide Web.

Recent research, however, suggests that studies on the document body alone may no longer be sufficient in understanding the language usages in our daily lives. A document, for example, is typically associated with multiple text streams. In addition to the document body that contains the bulk of the contents, there are also the title and the filename/URL the authors choose to name the document. On the web, a document is often linked with anchor text or short messages from social network applications that other authors use to summarize the document, and from the search logs we learn the text queries formulated by the general public to specify the document. A large scale studies reveal that these text streams have significantly different properties and lead to varying degrees of performance in many NLP applications (Wang *et al*, 2010, Huang *et al*, 2010). Consequently from the statistical modeling point of view, these streams are better regarded as composed in distinctive languages and treated as such.

This observation motivates the creation of Microsoft Web N-gram corpus in which the materials from the body, title and anchor text are made available separately. Another notable feature of the corpus is that Microsoft Web N-gram is available as a cross-platform XML Web service[1] that can be freely and readily accessible by users through the Internet anytime and anywhere. The service architecture also makes it straightforward to perform on

[1] Please visit http://research.microsoft.com/web-ngram for more information.

Proceedings of the NAACL HLT 2010: Demonstration Session, pages 45–48,
Los Angeles, California, June 2010. ©2010 Association for Computational Linguistics

demand updates of the corpus with the new contents that can facilitate the research on the dynamics of the Web.[2]

2 General Model Information

Like the Google N-gram, Microsoft Web N-gram corpus is based on the web documents indexed by a commercial web search engine in the EN-US market, which, in this case, is the Bing service from Microsoft. The URLs in this market visited by Bing are at the order of hundreds of billion, though the spam and other low quality web pages are actively excluded using Bing's proprietary algorithms. The various streams of the web documents are then downloaded, parsed and tokenized by Bing, in which process the text is lowercased with the punctuation marks removed. However, no stemming, spelling corrections or inflections are performed.

Unlike the Google N-gram release which contains raw N-gram counts, Microsoft Web N-gram provides open-vocabulary, smoothed back-off N-gram models for the three text streams using the CALM algorithm (Wang and Li, 2009) that dynamically adapts the N-gram models as web documents are crawled. The design of CALM ensures that new N-grams are incorporated into the models as soon as they are encountered in the crawling and become statistically significant. The models are therefore kept up-to-date with the web contents. CALM is also designed to make sure that duplicated contents will not have outsized impacts in biasing the N-gram statistics. This property is useful as Bing's crawler visits URLs in parallel and on the web many URLs are pointing to the same contents. Currently, the maximum order of the N-gram available is 5, and the numbers of N-grams are shown in Table 1.

Table 1: Numbers of N-grams for various streams

	Body	Title	Anchor
1-gram	1.2B	60M	150M
2-gram	11.7B	464M	1.1B
3-gram	60.1B	1.4B	3.2B
4-gram	148.5B	2.3B	5.1B
5-gram	237B	3.8B	8.9B

[2] The WSDL for the web service is located at http://web-ngram.research.microsoft.com/Lookup.svc/mex?wsdl.

CALM algorithm adapts the model from a seed model based on the June 30, 2009 snapshot of the Web with the algorithm described and implemented in the MSRLM toolkit (Nguyen et al, 2007). The numbers of tokens in the body, title, and anchor text in the snapshot are of the order of 1.4 trillion, 12.5 billion, and 357 billion, respectively.

3 Search Query Segmentation

In this demonstration, we implement a straightforward algorithm that generates hypotheses of the segment boundaries at all possible placements in a query and rank their likelihoods using the N-gram service. In other words, a query of T terms will have 2^{T-1} segmentation hypotheses. Using the famous query "mike siwek lawyer mi" described in (Levy, 2010) as an example, the likelihoods and the segmented queries for the top 5 hypotheses are shown in Figure 1.

Figure 1: Top 5 segmentation hypotheses under body, title, and anchor language models.

As can be seen, the distinctive styles of the languages used to compose the body, title, and the anchor text contribute to their respective models producing different outcomes on the segmentation task, many of which research issues have been explored in (Huang *et al*, 2010). It is hopeful that the release of Microsoft Web N-gram service can enable the community in general to accelerate the research on this and related areas.

4 Word Breaking Demonstration

Word breaking is a challenging NLP task, yet the effectiveness of employing large amount of data to tackle word breaking problems has been demonstrated in (Norvig, 2008). To demonstrate the applicability of the web N-gram service for the work breaking problem, we implement the rudimentary algorithm described in (Norvig, 2008) and extend it to use body N-gram for ranking the hypotheses. In essence, the word breaking task can be regarded as a segmentation task at the character level where the segment boundaries are delimitated by white spaces. By using a larger N-gram model, the demo can successfully tackle the challenging word breaking examples as mentioned in (Norvig, 2008). Figure 2 shows the top 5 hypotheses of the simple algorithm. We note that the word breaking algorithm can fail to insert desired spaces into strings that are URL fragments and occurred in the document body frequently enough.

baseratesoughtto Go

Phrase	LgProbability
base rates ought to	-11.27741
base rate sought to	-13.05057
baserate sought to	-14.4719
bas eratesough tto	-15.80559
bas eratesough t to	-16.01948

smallandinsignificant Go

Phrase	LgProbability
small and insignificant	-7.619725
smalland insignificant	-11.29643
small and in significant	-11.95384
s mall and insignificant	-14.1509
small an d insignificant	-14.51587

ginormousego Go

Phrase	LgProbability
ginormous ego	-9.646846
ginormous e g o	-13.63481
ginormouse go	-13.67101
ginormous e go	-15.15745
ginor mouse go	-15.43486

whorepresents Go

Phrase	LgProbability
who represents	-6.325181
whorepresents	-8.504251
whore presents	-9.705132
who represent s	-10.01388
who re presents	-10.29962

therapistfinder Go

Phrase	LgProbability
therapist finder	-8.399693
therapistfinder	-8.413392
the rapist finder	-10.2266
t herapistfinder	-12.53118
the rapistfinder	-12.53118

expertsexchange Go

Phrase	LgProbability
experts exchange	-7.010035
expertsexchange	-8.64951
expert sex change	-9.461636
expert s exchange	-9.509128
expert sexchange	-9.904957

penisland Go

Phrase	LgProbability
pen island	-8.247343
penisland	-8.582563
penis land	-9.35071
pen is land	-11.01801
penis l and	-11.71333

Figure 2: Norvig's word breaking examples (Norvig, 2008) re-examined with Microsoft Web N-gram

Two surprising side effects of creating the N-gram models from the web in general are worth noting. First, as more and more documents contain multi-lingual contents, the Microsoft Web N-gram corpus inevitably include languages other than EN-US, the intended language. Figure 3 shows examples in German, French and Chinese (Romanized) each.

gutenmorgen Go

Phrase	LgProbability
guten morgen	-7.971644
gutenmorgen	-9.321593
gut en morgen	-12.23253
gu ten morgen	-12.23306
gute n morgen	-12.52743

parlezvousfrancais Go

Phrase	LgProbability
parlez vous francais	-7.901024
parlezvous francais	-11.01565
parlez vousfrancais	-11.23517
parlezvousfrancais	-11.41711
parle z vous francais	-14.1426

wangfujingdajie Go

Phrase	LgProbability
wangfujing dajie	-8.801876
wangfujing da jie	-10.41473
wangfujingdajie	-11.16184
wangfujing daji e	-14.98702
wangfujingda jie	-18.14984

Figure 3: Word breaking examples for foreign languages: German (top), French and Romanized Chinese

Secondly, since the web documents contain many abbreviations that are popular in short messaging, the consequent N-gram model lends the simple word breaking algorithm to cope with the common short hands surprisingly well. An example that decodes the short hand for "wait for you" is shown in Figure 4.

w84u Go

Phrase	LgProbability
w8 4 u	-10.0969
w84u	-10.27723
w 84u	-10.69117
w 84 u	-10.7444
w 8 4 u	-11.06896

Figure 4: A word breaking example on SMS-style message.

References

Thorsten Brants and Alex Franz. 2006. *Web 1T 5-gram Version 1*. Linguistic Data Consortium, ISBN: 1-58563-397-6, Philadelphia.

Michel Banko and Eric Brill. 2001. Mitigating the paucity-of-data problem: exploring the effect of training corpus size on classifier performance for natural language processing. *Proc. 1st Internal Conference on human language technology research*, 1-5, San Diego, CA.

David Graff and Christopher Cieri. 2003. *English Gigaword*. Linguistic Data Consortium, ISBN: 1-58563-260-0, Philadelphia.

Jian Huang, Jianfeng Gao, Jiangbo Miao, Xiaolong Li, Kuansan Wang, and Fritz Behr. 2010. Exploring web scale language models for search query processing. In *Proc. 19th International World Wide Web Conference (WWW-2010),* Raleigh, NC.

Steven Levy, 2010. How Google's algorithm rules the web. *Wired Magazine*, February.

Patrick Nguyen, Jianfeng Gao, and Milind Mahajan. 2007. MSRLM: a scalable language modeling toolkit. *Microsoft Research Technical Report MSR-TR-2007-144.*

Peter Norvig. 2008. Statistical learning as the ultimate agile development tool. *ACM 17th Conference on Information and Knowledge Management Industry Event (CIKM-2008),* Napa Valley, CA.

Kuansan Wang, Jianfeng Gao, and Xiaolong Li. 2010. The multi-style language usages on the Web and their implications on information retrieval. In submission.

Kuansan Wang, Xiaolong Li and Jianfeng Gao, 2010. Multi-style language model for web scale information retrieval. In *Proc. ACM 33rd Conference on Research and Development in Information Retrieval (SIGIR-2010)*, Geneva, Switzerland.

Kuansan Wang and Xiaolong Li, 2009. Efficacy of a constantly adaptive language modeling technique for web scale application. In *Proc. IEEE International Conference on Acoustics, Speech, and Signal Processing (ICASSP-2009)*, Taipei, Taiwan.

Author Index

Association for Computational Linguistics
209 N. Eighth Street
Stroudsburg, Pennsylvania 18360

CURRAN ASSOCIATES INC
proceedings.com